CAREERS IN CONSUMER PROTECTION

Covers the full spectrum of careers in the broad field of consumer protection, particularly in the variety of city, state, federal and private agencies that look after the interests of the consumer, and includes the related field of safety design and testing. Opportunities in this exciting and rapidly expanding field have the added attraction of personal fulfillment and a chance to help build a better world for tomorrow.

SCIENCE BOOK ASSOCIATES' TITLES

ATOMIC ENERGY FOR HUMAN NEEDS
by David Reuben Michelsohn, with Editorial Supervision by Science Book Associates

CAREERS IN CONSUMER PROTECTION
by Sterling McLeod and the editors of Science Book Associates

CAREERS IN ENVIRONMENTAL PROTECTION
by Reed Millard and the editors of Science Book Associates

THE CITIES IN TOMORROW'S WORLD
Challenges to Urban Survival
by David Reuben Michelsohn and the editors of Science Book Associates

CLEAN AIR—CLEAN WATER FOR TOMORROW'S WORLD
by Reed Millard and the editors of Science Book Associates

HOUSING IN TOMORROW'S WORLD
by David Reuben Michelsohn and the editors of Science Book Associates

HOW WILL WE FEED THE HUNGRY BILLIONS?
Food for Tomorrow's World
by Nigel Hey and the editors of Science Book Associates

HOW WILL WE MEET THE ENERGY CRISIS?
Power for Tomorrow's World
by Reed Millard and the editors of Science Book Associates

HOW WILL WE MOVE ALL THE PEOPLE?
Transportation for Tomorrow's World
by Sterling McLeod and the editors of Science Book Associates

MEDICINE AND HEALTH CARE IN TOMORROW'S WORLD
by Madelyn Wood and the editors of Science Book Associates

NATURAL RESOURCES
Will We Have Enough for Tomorrow's World?
by Reed Millard and the editors of Science Book Associates

THE OCEANS IN TOMORROW'S WORLD
How Can We Use and Protect Them?
by David Reuben Michelsohn and the editors of Science Book Associates

CAREERS in CONSUMER PROTECTION

by **STERLING McLEOD**
and the editors of
Science Book Associates

photographs

Julian Messner
New York

Published by Julian Messner, a Division of Simon & Schuster, Inc. 1 West 39 Street, New York, N. Y. 10018. All rights reserved.

 # 5823

Library of Congress Cataloging in Publication Data

McLeod, Sterling.
   Careers in consumer protection.

   Bibliography: p. 167
   SUMMARY: Outlines the need for protection in matters concerning the consumer's safety, money, and consumption of foods and drugs and discusses the variety of careers in this field.
   1. Consumer protection—Vocational guidance— Juvenile literature. [1. Consumer protection—Vocational guidance] I. Science Book Associates. II. Title.
HC79.C63M3   381'.3   74-7591
ISBN 0-671-32691-0
ISBN 0-671-32692-9 (lib. bdg.)

Printed in the United States of America

Contents

Contents

FOREWORD

The Consumer Revolution—
Career Challenge

In the early 1960s, President John F. Kennedy proposed a bill of rights for consumers. Every American, he stated, has:

The right to safety: to be protected against the marketing of goods which are hazardous to health or life.

The right to be informed: to be protected against fraudulent, deceitful or grossly misleading information, advertising, labeling or other practices, and to be given the facts he needs to make informed choices.

The right to choice: to be assured access, wherever possible, to a variety of products and services at competitive prices, and, in those industries in which competition is not workable and government regulation is substituted as an assurance of satisfactory quality, at fair prices.

The right to be heard: to be assured that consumer interests will receive full and sympathetic

9

consideration in the formulation of government policy and fair, expeditious treatment in administration tribunals.

This statement by the president of the United States marked another milestone in what has been called "the consumer revolution." That revolution, which developed through the 1960s as Ralph Nader and other consumer advocates made themselves heard, is still gaining momentum. Almost daily, headlines reflect the steadily widening scope of government and business activities that concern consumers: 500,000 AUTOMOBILES RECALLED . . . DANGEROUS DRUG BANNED . . . MEAT PLANT CONDEMNED . . . HOME IMPROVEMENT FRAUD EXPOSED . . . REPAIR RACKET REVEALED . . . SALE OF DEADLY TOYS STOPPED . . . NEW CONSUMER AGENCY PLANNED.

There are a number of developments in the field of consumer protection that point up its growth and potential for meaningful careers:

An increase in the number of federal agencies dealing with consumer interests. Examples are the Product Safety Commission and the Highway Safety Commission. These new agencies deal with areas of consumer welfare that are regulated by new laws and regulations, such as the Flammable Fabrics Act. The Office of Consumer Affairs, predecessor to the new Consumer Protection Agency, is the most important example.

Extension of the powers of existing agencies to cover new aspects of consumer welfare. Examples are the U.S. Department of Agriculture's requirement for indicating the nutritional value of meat, and the Food and Drug Administration's requirements limiting the use of added vitamins in food products.

Establishment of many state, regional, county and city agencies designed to protect consumers. All states now have some kind of consumer protection agency, and many smaller governmental units are also setting them up.

Extension of the capabilities of private consumer protection organizations. Consumer's Union, the leading testing organization, is an example. It has increased the number of consumers it serves through its publication, *Consumer Reports,* and has set up an organization which brings suit on behalf of consumer groups. Another example is the expansion of Better Business Bureaus, some of which are operating mobile units to investigate consumer complaints. A computer network now links 150 local bureaus.

Establishment of a large number of new consumer membership organizations that engage in various kinds of consumer protection. Examples are the Chicago Area Consumer Advisory Board and the San Francisco Consumer Action Organization.

11

CAREERS IN CONSUMER PROTECTION

The increasing concern of business and industry for the consumer's welfare. Many trade associations, with memberships made up of companies in specific fields, have set up departments to help member companies better meet consumer needs. The National Business Council for Consumer Affairs includes a broad range of industries.

Widespread action on the part of business concerns and industries which have recognized that providing better merchandise and service is in the interest, not only of the consumer, but of the company as well. Hundreds of companies have set up customer relations departments and have even established hot lines the customer can use to call headquarters with the assurance that he will get some action. Still more companies are taking the "consumer approach" to their products, redesigning them in an effort to improve their quality and safety. Tough new federal and state regulations have forced many companies to take this step; other businesses are voluntarily making changes that benefit consumers.

Consumer protection is, indeed, a growing field, destined to reach proportions undreamed of just a few years ago. In that growth lies both challenge and opportunity for anyone who would like to have a vital career protecting the health, safety or money of his or her fellow consumers.

THE CHALLENGES

1. Protecting the Consumer's Safety

Protecting the safety of consumers by making products safer is one of the most exciting challenges in the broad field of consumer protection. Just how great a challenge it is can be shown by the staggering toll of accidents on the highway and in the home.

The National Highway Traffic Safety Commission estimates that in the United States the "social cost"— a term used to cover not only the cost of physical damage, but the time of police officers and the lost earnings of accident victims—of automobile accidents is upwards of *fifty billion* dollars a year. In human terms, the annual loss is even more frightful—2,000,000 people injured seriously enough to suffer ill effects beyond the day of the accident, and approximately 55,000 killed.

Home hazards, although they receive much less publicity than auto accidents, also pile up a disastrous record. Each year, according to the Consumer Product Safety Commission, 20,000,000 Americans are injured and 30,000 killed by products commonly found in the home.

Of course, not all of the accidents represented in these chilling statistics are caused by weaknesses in the products involved. However, a substantial number of them are—a far greater number, the federal agencies charged with consumer safety are finding out, than has been generally recognized. The engineers, scientists and technicians working with these organizations are dedicated to the idea that by improving machines, devices and products they can make our world a far safer place.

Can They Be Made Safe At Any Speed?

When Ralph Nader tossed his bombshell under the tires of the automobile industry in 1965, he pushed along the trend toward making cars and highways safer. In the eight-year period following the first publication of Nader's scathing book, *Unsafe at Any Speed,* more than *thirty-six million cars* were recalled by the manufacturers for the correction of defects. Some of these flaws were minor and probably would not have caused accidents. Others were major defects, such as faulty steering systems that could have failed and brakes that wouldn't stop the car. Partly as a direct result of the Senate hearings on automobile safety—often called "the Nader hearings"—

the National Highway Traffic Safety Administration came into being. This federal agency has the authority to compel the automobile industry to adopt new safety equipment.

Two important safety features found in most post-1967 cars indicate the kind of improvements that can be made. These two features, the energy-absorbing steering column and the high penetration resistant windshield, are credited with lowering the accident fatality rate, which began to drop immediately after they were introduced in 1967. The energy-absorbing steering column saves lives by reducing injury to the driver's chest in a frontal crash. The safety windshield, which is made with a layer of tough plastic between two layers of glass, keeps an occupant's head from going through the glass in a crash.

The goal of the NHTSA is to build into cars a greater degree of "crash survivability" than they possess today. Seat belts and shoulder harnesses go a long way toward this objective. One study indicates that lap belts have reduced serious and fatal injuries by 43 per cent. In another study of 228 actual crashes in which occupants were wearing both lap and shoulder belts, there were no fatalities—except in the cases where a colliding car or tree actually entered the passenger compartment.

The trouble with these effective safety devices is that people just don't use them. A study made by the Insurance Institute for Highway Safety revealed that only 16.3 per cent of the drivers in recent model cars equipped with seat belts actually use them; only 6.5 per cent used both lap and shoulder belts. Many experts believe that 10 per cent is a reasonable national figure for the number of people who use seat belts.

Safety campaigns urging people to "buckle up" evidently have little effect. Setups which force at least the driver to fasten lap and shoulder belts before he can start the car have met with wide disapproval. Many drivers with newer cars equipped with these ignition-linked devices have had them removed. Others have disconnected the warning buzzer that indicates a driver has failed to fasten his safety belt.

These difficulties with belts have led the NHTSA to turn to another device—the air cushion or safety air bag. These air bags are kept in a deflated state in a recess in the steering column. If a car is hit with an impact equal to that resulting from slamming into a brick wall at eight miles an hour, the bag instantly inflates. It holds the passenger behind it gently and firmly, pushing him back against the seat long enough to cushion him against the shock. The bag then deflates. The entire process, from the moment a delicate electronic sensor responds to the collision to the moment of deflation, takes less than half a second. A passenger or driver thrown forward by the impact has moved only a few inches before he meets the inflating bag ballooning out toward him.

Is the air bag the best solution? There are many doubters among safety experts and engineers. The bags were to have been made required equipment on 1973 cars, but problems with them made the NHTSA keep moving the date ahead, with the latest projected year being 1976. Engineers are fearful that the bags won't work too well if the passenger does not happen to be facing straight ahead. In addition, experiments with dummies show that a badly twisted neck or a wrenched back could result when the passenger bounces back from the bag. Another worry that troubles auto makers is the question of whether they can make the bags 100 per cent reliable. Can they in all certainty prevent a bag from inflating when it shouldn't? And what if the delicate sensor goes out of order and doesn't cause the bag to inflate in an actual crash?

Another question that troubles the automotive engineers is that of whether seat belts are needed to go with the air bags. This is a matter of argument. One engineer says flatly, "Air bags aren't any good unless you have lap belts with them." The argument is that lap belts will help solve the problem of the out-of-position passenger and cut the chance of rebound injury. Critics point out that air bags aren't much help in many kinds of crashes, such as side-impact and rear-end collisions. Seat belts, however, will work on any type of crash, not just the frontal crashes which account for about 40 per cent of all fatal crashes.

Still another problem is the one that arises when more than one impact occurs in a single crash, as is often the case. A possible solution to this is a bag that will re-inflate almost instantly. However, to make a bag that can do this would be complicated and expensive, and it would still not solve the question of dependability.

The difficulties connected with the air bag illustrate the point that, as one engineer puts it, "nothing is really simple in automobile safety."

This point is even more vividly illustrated by the efforts to create a "safety car." Many safety experts advocate "people packaging." This idea involves modifying the car itself to make it safer. Dr. William Haddon, a noted crash authority, compares the situation to that of sending a china teacup by mail. If you want to be sure the cup gets to its destination unbroken, you assume that postal authorities are going to drop the package and toss it around. So you protect the cup with adequate wrappings.

This is the concept behind the NHTSA's special program—the Experimental Safety Vehicle. A number of companies are working on the ESV. One scheme is to enclose the passengers in a "safety capsule." The idea is that, in the event of a collision, the engine—instead of being rammed into the car to crush the passengers—will be forced downward by the capsule's shape, which is like the prow of a boat. The capsule itself is made very strong. But the other parts of the car are made weak, so that, as they collapse, they absorb more of the energy of the collision than if they resisted it. There would be much less force left to be imparted to the capsule.

Many other safety features are being incorporated in the various versions of the ESV, some of which may be adapted to production cars. However, a big problem looms ahead. As one engineer working on an ESV puts it, "I'm afraid we're headed for an economic stone wall."

A *Fortune* magazine report explains, ". . . as cars for consumers the ESVs are all wrong. . . . They demonstrate that in the thrust for passive crash survivability, the added weight and cost and intrusion on passenger space will make automobiles unmarketable before making the occupants safe in collisions at highway speeds."

Of course, ordinary passenger cars can have a lot more safety features built into them without paying the heavy penalty in weight and cost that would seem to rule out the ESV approach. Energy-absorbing bumpers, roll bars and reinforced passenger compartments can be used without much redesign of the whole car. Simply using better materials and workmanship to avoid the dangerous defects that have made many automobiles unsafe in the past can result in a big improvement.

Many engineers feel that emphasizing crash survivability is the wrong approach. "Let's do more to *prevent* crashes," they say.

One promising approach to crash prevention is simply to provide better warning of the approaching danger of a crash. Experts have concluded that well over half of all collisions involving more than one vehicle occur because drivers "do not obtain adequate information concerning the movement of vehicles ahead of them." One step toward giving drivers better information could be to change the rear lighting systems of cars.

Imagine that you're driving along, close behind another car, and the driver ahead jams on his brakes. But since the brake light is located in the same bank as the tail lights, you may not notice the fact that it's the brake light that's on.

A simple solution to this situation would be to give the brake light a place by itself, perhaps in the center of the car and perhaps much higher on the car than just above bumper level. If the light was also made brighter than present brake lights, its attention-getting quality would be greatly increased. The split second of extra warning that you had better jam on *your* brakes could make the difference between crash or no-crash. This innovation alone might eliminate many rear-end collisions.

Technology may help diminish the greatest driving hazard of all—the drunk driver. Studies indicate that in the mid-1970s, one-half of all fatal accidents in the United States were caused by drivers who are intoxicated! Tougher laws and driver education can help, but many experts feel that the best approach is a mechanical one. Automotive engineers have produced a device on which the driver must punch out numbers in a certain sequence before the ignition of the car will turn on. A sober person has no difficulty in quickly tapping out the code; someone too drunk to drive a car could not do it correctly. Installation of this equipment is a matter of heated controversy. Should *all* drivers have to go through this extra procedure to keep drunk drivers off the road? Many drivers feel that this is an unwarranted invasion of their rights.

This is another illustration of the fact that nothing is simple when it comes to making automobiles safer to drive.

Danger In The Home

The National Product Safety Commission, set up in 1973, says that there are more than 10,000 different products in common use in the daily lives of American consumers. The task of this federal agency is to check out these products and make sure they are safe. (Literally thousands of products present hazards to their users—hazards that can maim and kill.)

"Most consumers think that a product is safe when they buy it in the store. 'It must be safe,' they argue, 'or they wouldn't allow it on the shelves.' When I ask them who this mysterious 'they' is, nobody seems to know," says Richard Simpson, first chairman of the commission. "The fact is, in many instances, there have been no government or tough industry standards for many, many products sold in this country."

High on the list of dangerous products are aerosol cans —cans which have the potentiality of becoming "aerosol bombs." Aerosol cans, of which more than two billion a year are used in the United States for a wide variety of products, contain propellants that provide the pressure to expel the product from the can. The cans are designed to operate most efficiently at a temperature of around 70° F. The pressure inside the can increases with temperature, and if the temperature gets high enough—generally about 120° F—the pressure will burst the can. When this happens, the container tears apart, hurling jagged pieces of metal considerable distances. The heating that causes this explosion can come from a variety of sources—hot water, sunlight, a heater or open flames.

Some typical accidents resulting from aerosol can explosions are described in a report prepared for the NPSC:

A woman discarded an empty can of insect repellent into a wastepaper fire. It exploded, and a piece of flying metal pierced her jugular vein. She died fifteen minutes later.

A child warmed an aerosol container in hot water to "jack up" the propellant. He then removed it from the water and shook it. The container exploded, and flying metal caused him to lose an eye and half of his lower jaw.

A woman put a can of hair spray on a gas-fired heater in her bathroom. It exploded and caused her death.

Studies show that consumers are not sufficiently aware

of the danger that lurks in aerosol cans. The danger has certainly not been clearly and emphatically indicated on the cans. By simply labeling the cans more clearly, the commission experts believe many injuries might be prevented. They propose wording that should appear on the can in "large, colorful type":

> On front of container:
> Caution: Contents Under Pressure. Read Precautions on Back Before Using.
> On back of container:
> DANGER: Contents of this Container are Under Pressure. Exposure to High Temperature May Cause Explosion. Keep Container at Room Temperature. Do Not Expose to Direct Sunlight. Do Not Place Near Radiators, Stoves or Other Sources of Heat. Do Not Place in Hot Water. Do Not Puncture Container. Do Not Throw into Fire or Incinerator. Do Not Place Near Flame. Keep Out of Reach of Children. This Container May Explode at Temperatures Above 120° F.

"Simply putting warnings on the cans isn't going to do the job," says a safety engineer working on the aerosol problem. "There are going to be accidents until we make the cans completely safe."

Making them safe is no easy task, but engineers have accepted the challenge. One approach is to make the cans strong enough to resist explosion even at high temperatures. Another is to make them out of plastic instead of metal. Flying pieces of plastic wouldn't do the damage done by shards of metal. Still a third approach is to devise a safety valve that will open automatically and release the propellant when the can reaches a dangerous temperature.

Another type of container that the aroused safety experts are tackling is the glass bottle. The NPSC has determined that 111,000 Americans each year require hospital emergency room treatment for glass container injuries. Half of these involve carbonated soft drink bottles. In fact, the commission reports that more injuries result from glass container accidents than from any other consumer product. One bottle out of every 100,000, the Commission asserts, is defective. Such defects can cause episodes like the one that occurred in a supermarket where an elderly woman was waiting to check out a bottle of ginger ale she was carrying. Suddenly it exploded, spraying glass.

Here, as in the case of aerosol cans, one solution is to make the bottles stronger. This might be done in a way that some bottle makers are already trying out—coating the bottles with a tough plastic. Only a small percentage of the 25 billion returnable bottles and the 20 billion nonreturnable ones filled each year had been protected in this way by 1974.

The contents of containers, rather than the containers themselves, are a major source of danger to children.

The commission points out that there are fifty or more dangerous chemicals that are kept around the house. They include over-the-counter medicines, such as the ubiquitous aspirin, and extend to extremely dangerous prescription medicines such as sleeping pills. Great progress has already been made toward keeping these items away from children. Under the Poison Packaging Act of 1970, passed after a long fight by consumer advocates, aspirin is now sold only in hard-to-open bottles.

It is proving a great deal harder to eliminate the menace of household cleaners. The danger of these products is particularly great because children, tempted by the pleasant lemon or lime scents of many modern cleaning chemicals, are more likely to drink them than they were the antiseptic-smelling compounds of the past. Yet many of these products are just as dangerous as earlier ones. In many instances, parents and doctors may not even get a chance to employ antidotes because the child has drawn the fluid into his lungs, producing "chemical pneumonitis," which can be fatal in a few minutes.

Senator Warren Magnuson (Washington), a lawmaker whose name is on many consumer protection bills, cites two examples of the dangers in seemingly safe household equipment:

When eight-year-old Andrea contracted pneumonia, the doctor prescribed a vaporizer. Purchasing a unit at a nearby drugstore, the child's parents read

27

the instructions carefully. They filled the unit with water at night, plugged in the electric cord and relied upon the booklet's say-so that the unit was safe to leave unattended. All went well at first. The parents were so pleased they bought another vaporizer of the same brand three years later when Andrea caught a cold. A few nights later they heard a terrifying scream. Andrea lay on the floor, scalded. The vaporizer had tipped off its stool. Andrea lived, but her stomach, legs and neck are scarred, her jaw deformed.

In a suburb outside New Orleans, the Rev. John B. Dryer and his wife shopped for a crib and found a lid-topped one that seemed just the thing to protect young Johnnie from mosquitoes. The baby slept in the crib for over a year. Then one Sunday Johnnie's mother gave him his bottle, snapped the lid on the crib and left him to his noon nap.

An hour later the child's father saw a horrible sight. Johnnie had pushed the snap open with his bottle, pitted his young strength against the heat-stretched plastic strap and strangled between the lid and the crib's edge.

These are extreme cases, to be sure. But scores of other kinds of household appliances present hazards just as great, endangering not only children but adults as well. Among the targets of the consumer protectors are a wide variety of electrical appliances that can shock and burn. Some that have been spotted by the NPSC include portable TV sets, electric heaters, electric fry pans and electric lamps.

An example of a danger in TV sets came to light when it was discovered that some sets were giving off harmful X-rays. This is a common hazard in color TV sets, but usually the amount of X-rays emitted is small. Not so with the sets in question—those made by one large appliance firm. They were found to be giving off 16,000 times the allowable level! The rays were directed at the floor, but that was exactly where they hit small children clustered close around the set. Over 150,000 of the dangerous sets were recalled, and the defect corrected.

When new appliances come on the market, they are more likely to present unusual and unexpected hazards. This is the case with the microwave oven, a device which cooks foods in a fraction of the time required for ordinary ovens. Is it possible that they will also cook the consumer? Tests made in 1973 by Consumers Union seemed to indicate that they could. All the ovens tested gave off some radiation through door seals. The amount of radiation in some models increased dangerously when a paper napkin was caught in the door, leaving a tiny crack. The test engineers revealed that in spite of the safety interlocks that supposedly made it impossible, some ovens could be operated with the doors open. The testers withheld recommendation for all of the fourteen makes tested.

Home craftsmen who use power tools have introduced

a major menace into the home. The National Safety Council reports nearly 650,000 injuries a year from this source. Many of these injuries result from carelessness, but experts have found that simple changes in the design of tools could eliminate most of them. Many bench saws, for example, are made without a guard which would prevent the common accident of sawing off a finger or two. In most saws, the wood being fed into them can be kicked back at high speeds, and this is another source of many injuries. Makers of saws are working to devise a guard that could prevent this from happening.

A demonstration of how a simple change can prevent injuries is the "chuck key keeper" on power drills. This little piece of plastic, which holds the chuck key on the electric cord, makes it necessary for the user to unplug the device if he wants to change the drill bit. Many accidents previously arose from leaving the drill plugged in.

Another piece of power apparatus that takes a high toll in home injuries is the power lawn mower. "On opening day of the grass-grooming season," says a commission report, "the rotary mower begins its work of trimming lawns, fingers and toes."

Whirling power motor rotors can lop off a whole set of toes in nothing flat. Whirling at 21,000 revolutions per minute at the blade tip, the rotor exerts a pressure of 10,000 pounds per square inch. The trouble usually comes when the mower hits a rock or some other obstruction, raising the mower so the rotor can hit the foot of the operator. Safety devices have been developed that can throw the motor out of gear if it hits an obstruction. An even simpler approach, a better rear guard on the mower, also can help eliminate this danger. Safety engineers trying to make the rotary mower less lethal also propose greatly reducing the speed of the rotor. It can, they believe, be reduced to less than 10,000 RPM, at which rate it would not present the danger it does at high speeds.

One important way of protecting the consumer is to make the products he uses fireproof, or at least fire resistant. Every year 12,000 Americans die from fires, most of them in the home, and 300,000 more are injured, many seriously. The financial loss runs over twelve billion dollars annually! In preventing injuries and death from fire, the safety experts are confronted with a situation similar to that which exists in the case of automobile accidents. While it is true that many fires are caused by consumer carelessness, the United States Commission on Fire Protection and Control points out that we cannot rely on reforming people. Instead, we must build fire-preventive qualities into materials and products.

A massive effort to do just that is underway at many research institutions, such as the Bureau of Standards and the Underwriters Laboratories. Their efforts are directed toward two goals—keeping fires from starting and slowing fires that do start. They are making great progress toward both goals by developing new chemicals that make formerly inflammable materials fireproof, or at least flameproof. This is no easy task in the case of building materials and home furnishings because, while many chemicals tested will not burst into flames, they do give off poisonous gases when they get hot. These gases must be added to a list of about 300 kinds of dangerous gases given off by untreated materials when they burn. In fact, a large percentage of fire victims are killed or injured, not by flames, but by the effects of harmful gases.

Ironically, one of the worst gas problems turned up in connection with a type of fire extinguisher. It was discovered that many fire extinguishers of the kind that were supposed to go off at high temperatures contain carbon tetrachloride. This chemical could put out fires. But, unfortunately, in the process it became hot and produced clouds of phosgene gas—a type of gas that burned the lungs of victims in World War I! Such fire extinguishers have been banned.

A high priority target in consumer safety is the elimination of the most horrifying of all fire hazards—inflammable fabrics. Every year 3,000 people die from flaming clothing; some 200,000 burn cases are traced to burning fabrics. All too typical is the case of a four-year-old child who went into the kitchen while his mother slept, climbed up on a counter and accidently turned on a gas burner. His inflammable pajamas burst into flame. The boy died in the hospital a few hours later. Some fabrics do not have to be exposed to flame to catch fire. A man coming in from the cold leaned against a space heater to get warmed up fast. Although he was in contact with the heater for "only a minute or so," his jacket caught fire and he was severely burned. A ten-year-old girl backed up against a bathroom space heater. Its hot surface set her robe afire.

Such tragedies are unnecessary, the NPSC says. The Flammable Fabrics Act of 1967 prohibits the use of certain kinds of synthetics in wearing apparel. Flameproofing compounds have been developed that can turn even highly inflammable cotton into a flameproof, heat-resistant material. The 1973 regulation requiring that only flameproofed materials be used in children's sleepwear will save the lives of many children. "But it is only a start toward what we must do to end flammable fabric injuries," says a Product Safety Commission member.

The consumer protectors who are trying to make the world a safer place for consumers have their hands full as they also tackle the task of making toys safe for children. They are forced to match wits with the ingenuity of toy makers who, along with inventing new toys, inadvertently invent a lot of new hazards. The case of "Vampire Blood" is an example. It sounds dangerous— and it was! When a toymaker made up tubes of a chemical that looked like blood, for use in playing gory games, a lot of parents ended up shuddering. The occasion for this shuddering was not the idea of a product called "Vampire Blood," however, but the fact that the red chemical in the tubes turned out to be contaminated with a pathogenic bacterium which caused sores if it came in contact with a cut or a child's mouth. No record of how many children were injured by this product was compiled, but a lot of it had been used up before the FDA recalled the one million tubes still on store shelves.

Another dangerous toy detected by the Product Safety Commission was a metal casting set. It made possible the "fascinating hobby of making beautiful and useful metal containers," according to the manufacturer. However, it also made possible a lot of painful burns. Safety engineers examining it found that the electrically heated device reached a heat of 800° F. Moreover, they found that it was inadequately wired so that, along with a burn, the young metal craftsman could get an electrical shock.

Other hazards spotted by investigators trying to enforce the Toy Safety Act of 1969 included a variety of potentials for injury. One of them was a blow gun which used plastic darts with needle points. A number of children sucked them into their lungs. Then there were the ball-shaped caps called "cracker balls." They seemed like a good idea to the makers—but not to the children whose teeth were knocked out by them. The caps looked just like candy, and a number of children thought that was what they were. The innocent-looking caps exploded in their mouths. Another particularly fiendish toy was a baby rattle held together by sharp metal prongs. It did not take a very strong-jawed baby to bite off the plastic rattle and expose himself to the knifelike metal.

Toy makers certainly do not want to injure and kill children. Safety experts believe that now that there are laws governing toy safety, all the large, reputable toy makers have gotten the message. "They're trying hard to make toys safe for young consumers," says Dr. Simpson of the Product Safety Commission. A consulting engineer adds, "It isn't all that hard. A technology that can make rockets and spacecraft can certainly make a safe toy."

Indeed, model rockets are a good example of how a responsible, consumer-conscious toy maker can make a safe product in a field where it would seem that there would be great danger in the product. Actually, safety was the whole idea behind the design of the modern preloaded model rocket. It came into being because of a hazard that existed when there were no commercial models on the market. A report prepared for the NPSC indicates the condition:

> By 1957, the space age had come into its own and with its advent came excitement and the desire among science-minded young people to join the space race by building their own rockets. Pandemonium broke loose in schools and backyards.

Equipped with only his own inadequate knowledge and household materials, the young scientist began to build. The simple combination of the heads from kitchen matches and an empty carbon dioxide cartridge was very popular. Sometimes it made a rocket, but more often it made a lethal bomb. The junior chemist concocted strange mixtures with strange properties, such as the capacity for igniting when shaken or dropped or on contact with water or air. Young persons lacking access to safety equipment, material, and knowledge killed themselves with grim regularity. "Basement bombing" in itself is uncontrollable and laws were ineffective to prevent dangerous experiments. The accident rate was more than seven times as great as that for automobile travel.

William Estes, a young engineer, saw the need for a rocket model—along with seeing a good business opportunity. He and his associates worked out a preloaded rocket which they put on the market. But they did not offer it for sale until they were, as Estes puts it, "One hundred-and-one percent sure that it was absolutely kid proof—adult proof, too!" The commercially made rockets —now numbering in the millions—have never injured anyone who used them!

2. Protecting the Consumer from Dangerous Foods

Every year the average American family of four eats two-and-a-half tons of food. It is a major task of consumer protectors to make sure that food—*all* of it—is safe to eat.

To carry out that responsibility, thousands of scientists, engineers, technicians, home economists, nutritionists and inspectors must be added to the hundreds of thousands already fighting to assure us a plentiful supply of pure food. Although the techniques of food protection are well established and many great successes have been achieved, the consumer cannot sit back with the relieved feeling that the battle for safe food is won. Many baffling problems remain to be solved—problems that challenge the skill and knowledge of veteran professionals and newcomers alike. The major targets for the food protectors are harmful organisms, food additives and chemical invaders.

CAREERS IN CONSUMER PROTECTION

The Fight Against Harmful Organisms

Keeping the thousands of organisms that are harmful to man out of the food he eats is a field of consumer protection that is really centuries old. However, we still have a long way to go. Organisms that get into food supplies account for 2,000,000 to 5,000,000 illnesses every year in the United States. The United States Public Health Service lists twenty-four different infectious diseases that can be transmitted through food and water. They include colds, septic sore throat, influenza, typhoid fever, diphtheria, tuberculosis, undulant fever and infectious hepatitis. Beyond the disease carriers are the organisms that create deadly poisons.

Long before anyone knew of the role of bacteria in food spoilage, men dried foods, froze them in the winter and pickled them in brine and vinegar. Canning, flash freezing, freeze-drying and irradiation with germ-killing rays are ways we preserve foods today. But the fight against bacteria goes on.

"Don't think it isn't a struggle," remarks a USDA food inspector. For example, one kind of organism—Salmonella—comes in at least 1,000 different strains. Named after Dr. D. E. Salmon, who first isolated it, it flourishes in many kinds of foods. In spite of all the efforts to keep it out of food supplies, this organism still accounts for most gastrointestinal illnesses in the United States. Food and Drug Administration inspectors have found Salmonella in many processed foods that were thought to be germ free, including cake mixes, dried milk, smoked fish, dried egg mixes, poultry and candies.

Another common organism that confronts the embattled food protectors is Staphylococcus. This small, sphere-shaped organism is widespread in the everyday world. Many animals carry Staphylococci, and they grow on hands, on arms, in hair and in the nasal tracts of humans. Most of the time they do not do any harm in these locations. However, if they get into foodstuffs, where they flourish, they create toxins which are harmful to people, causing acute gastrointestinal distress. In food processing, proper sanitary precautions will keep staph out of food products, and the proper amount of heat will kill them if they do get into food.

It is no easy task for food scientists to pin the guilt on staph, as is demonstrated by a typical case in which a shipment of dried milk appeared to be responsible for an outbreak of food poisoning. However, microscopic examination of the suspected milk powder showed no sign of the organisms. That was not surprising, for the toxins they create do not show up visually—being colorless, odorless, tasteless and, of course, motionless. Even without the chemical tests that revealed the cause, the investigator was able to employ some detective work to find out the trouble.

A checkup of procedures revealed there had been no letdown in the proper precautions during the drying process. Plenty of heat had been applied. The staph had gotten into the whole milk *before* it was dried. The mistake was that of holding the whole milk for several hours at room temperature when it should have been refrigerated. During this period the staph had multiplied. The organisms themselves were duly destroyed when the milk was heated and dried, but the toxins, which are not affected by that amount of heat, remained.

Another bacterial enemy is one only recently pinpointed as a dangerous organism. *Clostridium perfringens* is a spore forming anaerobe—that is, a bacterium that grows without oxygen. For a long time food scientists did not think of this very common organism as being harmful. But today they know that—under certain circumstances—if it gets into food, it can present real hazards when the food gets to the home kitchen. The fact that it is widespread in many foods has been demonstrated by surveys such as that conducted by the FDA in one community. *C. perfringens* was found to be present in 45 per cent of the meats purchased at random in local retail stores!

Ordinarily these organisms would be destroyed in the cooking process. As a USDA report indicates,

Foods most frequently associated with outbreaks of food poisoning due to *C. perfringens* are meats, including fowl, and gravies that have been cooked and allowed to cool slowly. The potential hazard appears to be from contamination after cooking. If the spores are introduced while the food is between temperatures of 158° and 176° F., these temperatures would . . . allow rapid germination. Extremely rapid growth would occur if the food was allowed to remain at temperatures between 110° and 116° F.

Microanerobic conditions (no available oxygen in one portion of a mixture which otherwise has oxygen) can be created in containers that are not sealed. When a pot of gravy is boiled, for example, oxygen is driven out of the gravy. Oxygen can now permeate the gravy only from the top of the container. Anerobic conditions could easily exist at the bottom of the pot if it were deep enough. The more viscous the food, the more difficult it is for the oxygen from the air to penetrate. Anerobic conditions are more likely to be created in deep pots than in shallow pans. A boned and rolled roast would be another example. Anerobic conditions would be created in the center of the roast itself.

These observations indicate the extreme importance of making sure that the organism *C. perfringens* be kept out of the food products in the first place. "We've got to try to keep this time bomb from being placed in the home kitchen," says an FDA inspector, adding, "but it's not easy."

The most frightening and publicized food-poisoning

menace that challenges the nation's food protectors is certainly *C. botulinum,* the bacteria that produces the dreaded botulism. This deadly relative of the much less dangerous *C. perfringens* is a spore-causing bacteria common in soil and water, and one which can all too easily be introduced into food products. Indeed, it is very common in raw fruits and vegetables. Here it does no harm whatsoever. The trouble comes when the spores get a chance to produce bacteria, which in turn produce a toxin so virulent that it has been estimated that a pinch of it could kill a million people and a few teaspoonfuls the entire population of the earth!

Fortunately for mankind, *C. botulinum* seldom gets a chance to flourish. It is the task of food scientists to see to it that it *never* gets a chance. Actually, the preventive is quite simple—just heat a food substance to at least 240° F. and keep it at that temperature for thirty minutes or more. That's all there is to it. But any departure from that basic procedure can invite tragedy.

Since the toxins from *botulinum* cannot develop without oxygen, the danger area lies chiefly in canned foods. Here the problem narrows down to improper heating after canning. (Most canned goods are cooked in their cans.) A frightening example occurred in canned soup in 1971. It began when Samuel Cochran, Jr., of Bedford Village, New York, was rushed to the hospital where he died. At first it was thought that the cause of his death was a stroke. Then the family doctor got a call from the Cochran home. Mrs. Cochran had been stricken with the same symptoms that had assailed her husband—weak and trembling arms and legs, blurred vision, slurred speech. The information sparked a grim warning in the mind of Dr. Henry Colmore. These were the symptoms of botulism!

Mrs. Cochran was able to tell the doctors that the night before she and her husband had eaten some canned vichyssoise. It had tasted bad, so they hadn't finished it. Public health officials and FDA investigators were notified, and the empty can was retrieved and analyzed—with the positive results that had been feared.

When investigators reached the plant in New Jersey where the soup had been canned, they found a dismaying situation. The soup in the deadly can had been part of a batch labeled V-141, a code indicating that it had been processed on the one-hundred-and-forty-first day of the year, May 21. In the V-141 batch there had been 6,500 cans. Every one of these cans would have to be considered suspect and somehow recalled from the approximately 28,000 wholesalers and retailers who might have received some of them and might still have some on their shelves. To complicate matters, the soups had been put out under various house brands rather than one company brand. Public announcements and calls by investigators eventually rounded up 4,000 of the cans.

Some of them, including four cans on the shelves of the store where the Cochrans had shopped, proved to be contaminated.

"It was just a miracle that nobody else died," said one of the FDA investigators. "It was sheer luck that no one else happened to use one of the contaminated cans."

At the factory, food scientists sought and found the cause of the near disaster. The canning company, an old established firm that had been in business for over a hundred years, had slipped up on the basic precaution against botulism. In processing the vichyssoise and some other kinds of soups, it had failed to heat the cans to the required 240° F. and to keep them there at that temperature the necessary half hour. The investigation turned up the shocking fact that the plant had not been inspected by FDA investigators for *four years!*

The Questionable Additives

Every day most Americans sit down to eat what has been referred to as a "chemical feast" of food additives. Each year over one billion pounds of nearly 2,000 different kinds of chemicals are added to hundreds of kinds of food. That averages out to five pounds of chemicals per person. These chemicals perform various functions, changing the appearance, texture, flavor and preservative qualities of the foods to which they are applied.

The question that confronts consumer protectors, particularly the nutritionists, scientists, technicians and inspectors who guard the purity of our food supply, is—how dangerous to human health are chemical additives? The fear is growing that in this "chemical feast" may lie more hazards than even the most cautious nutritionists and medical authorities have believed.

Nutritionist Beatrice Trum Hunter, in her book, *Consumer Beware!*, gives this description of the dangerous potential of chemicals in food:

> Some additives produce chemical changes in the food itself by altering its biological structure. Others, which produce derangements in the human system, are so insidious that they do not become apparent until long after the original exposure. Because of this, they may not even be suspected as the original instigator of trouble.
>
> The fundamental biological mechanism of the body may be affected in ways scarcely appreciated at present. One of the earliest signs of harm may be the enlargement of vital organs, accompanied by microscopic changes that can be detected by a trained pathologist. Frequently, the enlarged liver, kidneys, and spleen of experimental animals are signs of damage. The increased size of these organs may be caused by stresses placed upon them to detoxify strange materials.
>
> Many chemical food additives interfere with the normal functioning of vitamins and enzymes, which

work closely together in the body. Vitamins play an important role in releasing energy for all physiological processes, including cell repair. Closely associated with them are the enzymes, which are the effective agents of the whole life-process. As long as each cell lives, it is continually being broken down and rebuilt. Energy is needed for this repair process. In a vitamin deficiency, where energy liberation is interfered with by the introduction of chemical food additives or other substances, the rebuilding process slows down or ceases; the cells die. When enough cells sicken and die, the body dies.

Injury or deterioration of the cells is recognized by physicians aware of vitamin-and-enzyme-deficiency symptoms. Patients are easily fatigued, show such symptoms as weakness, constipation, loss of appetite, headache, disturbance of sleep, excessive irritability, depression, inability to concentrate, queer feelings in the fingers and toes, burning tongue, gas, and many other odd bodily sensations. These symptoms may be classified vaguely as nervousness, neurasthenia or imagination, when in reality they may stem from impairment of the vitamin-enzyme system of the body.

Medical authorities and researchers have suggested that losses or deficiencies of enzymes lead to many diseases. Commonly used chemical food additives such as sulphur dioxide, sodium nitrate, food dyes, certain hormones used to stimulate plant and animal growth, antibiotics used in food production, fluorides used in processing water, and pesticides are all acknowledged enzyme destroyers. Adverse effects can occur even when the chemicals are present in exceedingly small amounts. For example, as little as 0.4 ppm of DDT inhibits a vital enzyme in human blood. Many chemical additives permitted in foods are present in amounts that adversely affect the body's enzymes. Some contaminants are harmful to animal life in amounts measured as parts per billion.

Catalase is one important enzyme found almost universally in living cells, not only in human beings, but also in animals, plants, and even in bacteria. This particular enzyme plays many vital roles. It is intimately related to cell respiration, and buffers the cell from toxic substances, infection, virus, radiation, and cancer. The normal cell maintains a specific balance of catalase and hydrogen peroxide. Catalase controls the hydrogen peroxide at a very low level, and converts it into oxygen and water. However, many substances, including some chemical food additives, destroy catalase. When this happens, the level of peroxide rises. This, in turn, results in the electron-transport system of the cell slowing down or stopping altogether. Cellular abnormalities may then develop, and the cell becomes predisposed to tumor formation and cancer.

Many scientists are worried about possible dangers that go beyond any immediate effects of chemicals on

47

the menu. They are concerned about the fact that many chemicals can react with and modify the composition of DNA molecules. These molecules make up the genetic blueprints that affect future generations. One possible result of such changes in the DNA can be damage to the mechanisms that affect cell growth, triggering the growth of tumors and cancers. Chemicals which have this effect are called *carcinogens*. Another effect on the DNA can be to injure mechanisms that direct the formation of bodily organs of the fetus, resulting in physical or mental defects in babies. The term *teratogens* is used to describe chemicals which have such effects. Chemicals of another class are called *mutagens,* indicating that their effect on the DNA molecules is to create mutated genes which are passed on to offspring. Such mutagens could have results extending to future generations.

"We have had some narrow escapes because of the use of additives that had no place in food," says George P. Larrick, former commissioner of the FDA.

Among the narrow escapes was the threat presented by Red Dye #1. This coal-tar derivative had been freely used in a variety of food products without adequate laboratory checks. When these checks were finally made, a typical experiment revealed that, of 250 rats fed varying amounts of Red Dye #1, 116 died. Many suffered liver damage and malignant tumors. Related types of dyes are still in use in this country and in some others. Of eighty-two different kinds of food dyes used in twenty-two countries, only one of the eighty-two is permitted in all twenty-two. This means that researchers in various countries have found some evidence against eighty-one of these dyes.

Other chemicals which turned out to be a threat to health were dulcin, an artificial sweetener that had been in use for half a century; coumarin, an artificial flavorer that had been used for seventy years; and hydrofluoric acid, used in processing beer. The use of a cobalt salt for improving the foamy appearance of beer was abandoned only after it had caused an estimated 100 heart attacks. A salt substitute, lithium chloride, was responsible for several deaths.

Perhaps the most famous case of a dangerous additive that seemed safe to begin with was cyclamate, an artificial sweetener. It came into wide use in the 1950s, in diet foods and low-calorie soft drinks. Hailed as a superior replacement for saccharine—it had no aftertaste —its use jumped by leaps and bounds. At the start of the 1960s, in one four-year period, the amount of it ingested by Americans rose from 5 million pounds to 15 million pounds.

It was some time before evidence of cyclamate dangers began to pile up. Even then the dangers were widely disputed by the industry which manufactured the substance and by the many food firms which used it. Among the discoveries about it were:

The finding by Dr. Marvin Legator, head of the FDA's cell biology branch, that in tests on rats, a chemical related to cyclamate produced breaks in the chromosome cells that form sperm and bone marrow cells.

Dr. Jaqueline Verrett of the FDA, examining thousands of chicken embryos, found that many had turned into deformed monsters after injection with cyclamate. One kind of cyclamate produced abnormalities in 15 per cent of the embryos; a cyclamate derivative produced abnormalities in 100 per cent.

A manufacturer of cyclamates found that rats fed with heavy doses of cyclamates developed bladder cancers.

The long struggle to ban cyclamates illustrates a question that has been argued hotly among scientists: what is a "safe dose"? In animal experiments, scientists have set up a standard of giving fifty times the amount of a substance recommended for human use. Other scientists argue that even this is not high enough, that the amount used in animal experiments should be 100 times that of the recommended human dose. There is much disagreement among scientists about this, along with widespread recognition that animal tests may not always be meaningful.

In the case of cyclamates, which were finally withdrawn from the market in September, 1970, after two decades of wide usage, the factor that brought about their removal was the demonstration that they did cause cancer in animals. The Food Additive Amendment of

1958—called the Delaney Clause (after Congressman James J. Delaney of New York)—flatly prohibits use of any substance that is "found after tests which are appropriate . . . to induce cancer in man or animals."

There is no simple solution to the problems created by the use of chemical additives. The problems cannot be solved by doing away with the additives. To be sure, some of them (such as those used simply to color food) are unnecessary and could be abandoned. Others serve essential purposes. This is particularly true of the preservatives. Many authorities, including some of the most concerned, defend their use.

"I'm not convinced . . . but that food completely free of additives may be more harmful than food properly protected by preservatives or anti-oxidants," says Dr. John H. Weisburger of the National Cancer Institute.

Medical men are impressed by the fact that, while the death rate from lung cancer, which may be attributed to cigarette smoking and air pollution, has gone up, the death rate from stomach cancer has steadily declined. In the period when additives came to be so widely used, the rate declined from thirty per 100,000 in 1930, to only eight per 100,000 in 1972. No scientist contends that this decline is due to the use of additives, but it seems to indicate to some that additives cannot be as harmful as many fear.

Science has made the discovery that nature herself has "added" many carcinogenic substances to commonly eaten foods. A chemical called patoulin is found in the juice of oranges; another, called thiourea, is found in cabbage; estrogen, the female hormone, is common in dairy products, eggs and leafy vegetables. All of these have been demonstrated to cause cancer in test animals. Nitrates, a class of chemicals widely used as preservatives, and challenged as dangerous, are present in spinach and many other vegetables.

Such facts make the task of those engaged in protecting our food much more difficult—and more challenging. Clearly, there is plenty of work ahead for tomorrow's scientists working in the food-additive sector of consumer protection.

The Chemical Intruders

In 1969 the Department of Health, Education and Welfare set up the Secretary's Commission on Pesticides and Their Relationship to Environmental Health. The committee, made up of eminent scientists from several fields, concluded that the long-term effects of pesticides presented many possible hazards that had been overlooked. The panel listed thirteen different pesticides as dangerous.

"Pesticides," said the committee report, "may represent an important potential teratogenic hazard. Therefore any teratogenic pesticide to which the population is exposed should be promptly identified so that appropriate precautions can be taken to prevent risk of human exposure."

The committee warned that people might be exposed to birth-defect-creating pesticides not only as residues in food and water, but in the air and in the home, where they are used in aerosol sprays. The committee's conclusion:

> To sum up, the field of pesticide toxicology exemplifies the absurdity of a situation in which 200 million Americans are undergoing life-long exposure, yet our knowledge of what is happening to them is at best fragmentary and for the most part inferential and indirect.

Actually, pesticides have not been held accountable for any human deaths or even injuries, so the consumer protectors investigating them have to face a major challenge. If pesticides are dangerous, the investigators must pinpoint the nature of their injury. If they are not dangerous to man, they must be exonerated from charges made against them, because it is generally agreed that chemical pesticides do serve a useful purpose in increasing our food supply. Alternative means of destroying pests by "biological warfare"—turning pest against pest, for example—are promising, but if the chemicals are safe to use, they can be an efficient means of pest and weed control.

Environmental scientists long ago established a strong

case against DDT, which was found to be building up in fish and birds. Its use was forbidden in many situations, and it is used little today. Other chemicals are on the spot, however, and may prove dangerous.

Finding out if these chemicals are safe is a long, complicated process. An example is the herbicide, 2,4,5-T, the defoliant used in Vietnam to destroy field plants and forests. Found in common use on American farms and, at one time, in backyard gardens and lawns as a weed killer, 2,4,5-T contains a chemical that is one of the most deadly substances on earth, TCDD. It has been described as being more like a nerve gas than a pesticide. The Herbicide Assessment Commission of the American Association for the Advancement of Science said of TCDD: "Its potential importance lies in the fact that it is exceedingly toxic, may be quite stable in the environment, and, being fat soluble, may be concentrated as it moves up the food chain into the human diet."

In spite of the obvious danger that lurked in 2,4,5-T, it became a subject of bitter controversy in the scientific world as to whether it should be banned. Results of animal tests were mixed, and they did not at first seem to indicate that the pesticide was hazardous if used carefully. Its use on food crops and in home garden compounds was prohibited at first, before it was finally determined that it should be banned for all use.

Carrying out tests in laboratories is comparatively simple. Far more complicated is the detective work involved in following the steps by which pesticides might get into the food chain. To realize just how complicated that can be, let Joseph W. Gentry of the Agricultural Research Service describe the Delta Study, a survey of three one-square-mile areas located in Mississippi and Arkansas:

A team led by a supervisory biologist was assigned to each location to conduct investigations in the field. First, the investigators laid out each area in plots or blocks for sampling purposes. Maps were diagramed to show where soil, water, crop, fish and other samples would be collected.

Then with the assistance of the farm operators, a detailed history for at least ten years was compiled upon kinds and amounts of pesticides used on each block since the introduction of DDT and of other chlorinated hydrocarbon insecticides.

Besides the pesticide-use history, the biologist and his crew began to record details of every pesticide application made in their areas. This meant keeping complex pest-control operations under constant surveillance—recording what was used, how it was applied, weather conditions and possible hazards to non-target organisms at time of application. They would continue these activities for the duration of the study. In the pest-control season that called for being on the job seven days in each week.

Since pesticides are known to move by air and water from one area to another, the biologist visited surrounding farms and cataloged the pesticides which were being used.

He was laying the groundwork, or establishing a base line against which the analytical results could be compared. In other words, to get any idea of the rate of buildup or breakdown of a pesticide in the soil, accurate figures were required on how much of the material had been applied.

While the field crews developed their plans of work, equipment for carrying out the program was arriving at the stations.

It was a collection of strange-looking items: five-gallon water bottles, bright new sample cans, light traps, weather equipment, sweep nets, tick drags, forage cutters, pumps, boots, dippers, sieves, shovels, ice-cream cups, portable freezers, jugs of alcohol to be used in insect traps and plastic bags of all shapes and sizes.

Everything was brand-new or sterilized. To work with residues at levels of sensitivity in parts per million and parts per billion, cleanliness is essential.

The central laboratory at Gulfport, Mississippi, was also gearing up at the same time for one of the largest analytical loads ever undertaken by a chemical laboratory in this country. More personnel, more equipment and more space were added. Chemical supplies by the barrelful were being trucked in instead of the customary quarts and gallons.

Suddenly, May came. Sampling had not yet started, but it was time for it. The cotton was up and growing and the soybeans were planted. Some weed killers had already been used, but no insecticide yet. A preseason sampling was needed at once.

The crews went at it. Technicians collected soil cores on a random pattern over each field, pasture and wildlife area. They used a two-inch diameter corer which they plunged into the ground to a depth of three inches. Each type of cropland was being sampled separately.

Cores from a field were deposited in a large collecting pail, then rubbed through a quarter-of-an-inch mesh screen. The material was passed through the screen again to insure thorough mixing. Stones, roots, grass and other debris that would not pass through the screen were discarded. A new, one-gallon paint container was then filled with the mixed, screened soil and sealed with an airtight lid.

The collector completed a data sheet, identifying the sample, and fastened it to the outside of the container. He cleaned up his equipment thoroughly and moved on to the next field. Soil samples were collected once each month during the first season.

The role of water as a carrier of pesticide residues is of prime interest to everyone studying the pesticide pollution problem.

Several of the Delta farms contained lakes, ponds and sloughs which got all their water from runoff from treated fields.

Analysis of the water and the mud in these sources would show the relative amounts of residues in soil, sediment and water. It would also furnish a base for comparison with levels found in the aquatic life, such as in turtles, frogs and fish.

Water was collected by using a bilge pump with an extended length of hose on the outlet.

This was a two-man job in the larger water sources. One man operated the pump while the other moved the five-gallon glass carboy and directed the water into the bottle. In deep water a boat was necessary.

Water was taken at several places at various depths over each water source. The bottle was carefully sealed after collection, labeled and taken to the laboratory as soon as possible for processing in order to prevent breakdown of the residue content.

Water was taken from ponds and other surface sources once each month and whenever a quick run-off occurred after rains. Wells were also sampled each month.

A sediment or mud sample was taken from the bottom of each pond, slough or stream each time a water sample was collected. The technician used a modified soil corer for this. He waded out through the water, plunging the corer at random into the bottom until he reached solid matter. The tool was withdrawn, and the mud ejected into a five-gallon container.

After a representative number of cores were collected, they were mixed by stirring, and a one-gallon portion taken off and prepared in the same manner as the soil sample. An extension was used on the handle of the sampler when sediment was collected from a boat in deep water.

Interspersed with the sampling of soil and water was the collection of plants and animals for residue analysis and insects for sorting and counting.

Crops were sampled at or near harvest. First came wheat, oats and hay. Later rice, cottonseed and soybeans would be taken.

Ten pounds of material, made up of plant tissues and seeds, were collected at random over the field; two samples came from each field or block. The material was placed in a plastic bag and sealed. If it was green or perishable, it was quick-frozen until facilities were provided at each of the field stations.

Forage was being sampled periodically, usually following the pesticide applications in nearby areas.

As the tons of samples came in each week, water was processed first. Each water sample was transferred to a larger bottle and 1,000 milliliters of redistilled pentane and ether (three-to-one ratio) were added as solvents. The sample was then put on a rotator and turned for twenty minutes. In this interval if pesticide residues were in the water, they would be extracted by the solvent. The solvent mixture was then drawn off in a bottle and the extract was ready for a chemical analysis.

In processing soil samples, a 300-gram portion was weighed out. This was placed in a half-gallon fruit jar and 600 ml. [milliliters] of redistilled hexane and isopropyl alcohol were added. The mixture was rotated for four hours on a wheel so that residues, if present, could be taken up in the solvent. The mixture was filtered and the solution washed twice with distilled water.

The extract containing the residues was then drawn off in a small bottle and placed in refrigeration. All samples were processed to the extract stage as soon as possible so they could be held for an indefinite period without significant deterioration or change in residue content.

After a portion of a soil or sediment sample was taken for processing, the remainder of the sample was placed in a separate building, which was especially reserved for this purpose, and held for later reference.

Perishable samples like green crop material and animals were kept frozen until they were extracted. Procedures different from those used for extracting soil and water samples were employed for processing biological samples, but the objective was the same: to "fix" the chemical content in an extract solution.

In the analytical laboratory a sample was subjected to one of several methods to determine its pesticide residue content both qualitatively and quantitatively. The sample was first injected into a highly sensitive gas chromatograph machine and then the findings were confirmed by the thin-layer chromatographic method as needed.

Other methods available in a well-equipped laboratory—like infrared spectrophotometry—were used, depending upon the type of pesticide that was involved.

Water samples were determined down to levels in parts per billion. Soil and other samples were analyzed in parts per million.

Chemical analysis of many different kinds of pesticide residues in many different kinds of samples of environmental media is a very complex and demanding job. If nothing unusual happens, a sample will require about three-man hours from the time it starts through the laboratory until the time the amounts of residue it contains are computed out. Whenever a problem sample turns up, which is about 30 per cent of the time, more than two days is required, on the average, to complete an analysis of the sample.

By the time more than 3,000 samples had been collected and analyzed in the Delta program, spring had come back again.

As scientists of the Agricultural Research Service, the Food and Drug Administration, the Public Health Service and other organizations continue their research, it is evident that the pesticide problem is complicated. Solving it is going to remain a challenge for many years —probably even for many decades—to come.

3. Protecting the Consumer from Dangerous Drugs

Every year Americans have nearly four billion prescriptions filled for various kinds of drugs.

Each year they buy about 100,000 different kinds of medicines that can be sold without prescription (over the counter)—including approximately 18,000 *tons* of aspirin, which is 225 tablets for every man, woman and child.

In addition to these nostrums they purchase about 15,000 different brands of such drug-based products as mouthwashes, toothpastes, shampoos and cosmetics.

The outpouring of remedies for the seemingly endless ills of mankind constitutes one of the greatest of all challenges to the consumer protectors in the sciences and in consumer protection and law enforcement agencies. The ability of giant pharmaceutical houses to turn out an avalanche of drugs is so great that the agencies designed to check them out cannot keep pace. Even the medical profession, which dispenses the drugs, is hard pressed to carry out its sworn duty to protect its patients.

Is a new drug a lifesaver—or is it a killer? Is it simply worthless, no more valuable than a sugar pill placebo? Are the old established drugs, which have been freely used for decades, as safe as they have always been thought to be? Are the nostrums, cosmetics and health products sold over the counter really as beneficial—or, more importantly, as safe—as the commercials say they are?

Are They Safe?

To find out if drugs are really safe requires far more vigilance and more elaborate and prolonged testing and study than was thought necessary, even in the recent past. Often drugs that showed great promise and seemed harmless turned out to have unexpected dangers in actual use.

A disturbing example is the frightening story of chloramphenicol, sold under the trade name of *Chloromycetin*. When Yale University researchers emerged with this new antibiotic, it was hailed as a brilliant triumph. And indeed it should have been, for it could do what none of the other antibiotics could. It knocked out the effects of typhoid fever, Rocky Mountain spotted fever and certain urinary tract infections. If its use had stopped

63

there, as the medical profession came to wish it had, it would have remained a standard drug for treating the approximately 10,000 people a year afflicted with the particular ailments it helped.

However, it didn't stop there. In a wave of overconfidence in the marvelous powers of the so-called "wonder drugs," doctors began prescribing Chloromycetin for other ailments. It was dispensed freely for common colds, sore throats, acne and various "superficial infections and dermatological conditions." Most doctors took the word of the pharmaceutical house that produced the drug that it was perfectly safe to use for these minor afflictions. Early tests had shown no side effects, and the drug seemed to be effective as a treatment for a host of different ills.

It was only after it had been given to millions of people that the distressing results began to come in. Quite simply, people began to die from certain unexpected effects of the drug on the bone marrow. The bone marrow would sometimes disintegrate and become unable to produce the blood cells that it normally does. The resulting "aplastic anemia" could be fatal, and it was in an unknown number of cases. A physician who had prescribed the drug for his own son wrote: "I might have done better had I taken a gun and shot him—at least he wouldn't have suffered."

The widespread use of this drug, with its dangerous

potential, could not occur in the 1970s as it did in the 1960s. The pharmaceutical houses themselves are more vigilant now, as they are required to be under new laws which demand far more complete checks. The law which enables the Food and Drug Administration to demand more care on the part of drug makers came into being as a result of the ultimate dangerous drug horror story— the thalidomide disaster.

Thalidomide, developed by a Swiss chemist in 1953, started out as a remarkably effective sleeping pill. It seemed to have no side effects, and it had a special virtue that made doctors all over Europe favor it: it was almost impossible to take an overdose of the drug. Soon after it was developed, it appeared under many brand names and was used by millions of patients.

As its use in Europe increased, an American pharmaceutical maker applied to the FDA for permission to introduce it in the United States. FDA scientists made a routine check, studied the reports from Europe and failed to find much evidence against use of the drug. However, one FDA researcher, Dr. Frances O. Kelsey, wasn't satisfied. She felt uneasy about the drug and thought that certain specific tests should be made in this country before it was released here. The old 1938 law under which she was operating hardly covered this situation, but she continued to hold up approval of the drug in spite of the insistent efforts of the pharmaceutical concern. By so doing, this courageous "consumer protector" saved hundreds, perhaps thousands, of American babies from the fate that met many in Europe.

It was 1961 when the full horror of the drug's consequences was at last revealed. For some years doctors had noticed an increase in the number of babies born with defective legs and arms, or with none at all. In Germany, in 1959, twelve cases were noted. In 1960, there were over 100; in 1961, several *thousand*. What could be causing this epidemic of terribly deformed babies? Finally many doctors in Europe came up with the dreadful answer: all of the mothers of these babies had taken thalidomide in the crucial months of their pregnancy.

In the United States, the news moved Congress to swiftly pass long-delayed amendments to the 1938 law, to give the FDA wider powers to control the introduction of new drugs. It placed the burden of proof on the drug manufacturers and required more extensive animal tests and reports to the FDA.

The amendments have proved to be a valuable safeguard, but they haven't, unfortunately, brought an end to the introduction of drugs that turn out to be dangerous. Although pharmaceutical houses now make far more extensive tests than formerly, some still do not carry out enough or conduct them properly. In some cases, companies may actually turn in false reports that may look authentic enough to fool the FDA.

An example of this is the detective story involving a

drug that was put forward as a medication to help reduce the cholesterol level of patients with heart ailments and hypertension. The company making it presented the results of tests to the FDA, which turned them down as inadequate. At last, however, the drug was conditionally approved on the basis of tests on monkeys, the results of which were presented to the FDA. The company recommended the drug to doctors in glowing terms, and thousands of doctors started prescribing it.

After some time, disquieting reports began to come in. The drug was having strange effects on some patients. Skin rashes, loss of hair and blurred vision were among the symptoms, with hints that liver damage was occurring. An FDA inspector in Cincinnati did not know about these reports when he learned that there was something strange about the monkey tests. The tip-off came from a former employee of the pharmaceutical company who had quit in disgust when he was asked to falsify reports of the monkey experiments. As he delved into the case, the FDA man discovered what had happened. Many of the monkeys used in the test had developed various symptoms which indicated dangers in the drug. Company researchers had altered the records to show that all the monkeys had exhibited these symptoms before the tests started. In the case of one very sick monkey, they had simply substituted a healthy monkey for the ailing one.

Even though such cases of outright fraud are comparatively rare, at least on the part of large pharmaceutical firms, the problem of keeping tabs on the effects of drugs on patients is enormously difficult. It is estimated that 10 per cent of all patients who take prescription medication suffer some kind of adverse reaction. Many of these people become sick enough to end up in the hospital. Some estimates run as high as 50 per cent, and various authorities state that the death toll from medication runs into the thousands every year!

"Beyond the measurable effects of medication," says an FDA investigator, "we are haunted by the possible effects on generations to come." There is evidence that more mutations are occurring, both physically and mentally. Some may be caused by radiation, some by environmental factors, but there is always the possibility that some may be resulting from the unsuspected effects of drugs.

"In the future," says an FDA spokesman, "we—meaning the medical profession, the pharmaceutical industry, and those of us charged with policing the field—will have to give far more consideration to long-term tests for drugs before we permit them to come into general use. We're dealing with too many unknowns. How would we feel if we introduce drugs that could bring about mutations, the evils of which will only show up in our grandchildren?"

The scientists and investigators out to protect the consumer from dangerous drugs are faced with another challenge. That is the problem of worthless drugs. As the consumer movement of the 1960s gathered momentum, the National Research Council of the National Academy of Sciences embarked on a long delayed study that "should have been made twenty-five years ago," as one noted scientist puts it. It is known as the Drug Efficacy Study. In conducting it, several hundred physicians and scientists undertook to rate about 3,000 standard drugs. These were products that had been used for many years, some for decades. The results of the study were startling, for they revealed that only 20 per cent of the old standbys were effective! Of the ten most commonly prescribed drugs, seven were either lacking in efficacy or were second or third choices over other drugs for use in the situations for which they were commonly prescribed. Many drugs rejected by the NRC have already been removed from pharmacists' shelves. One large pharmaceutical company had twenty-five of its products eliminated, another twenty-three. Many other firms had ten or more candidates for the discard list.

"And these won't be the last," warns an FDA inspector. "We'll have a continuing job cutting out the drugs that don't do the job they're supposed to do."

Over-the-Counter Menaces

The same charges made against drugs that are doctor-prescribed can also be made against a host of medical products sold over the counter in drugstores and supermarkets. To be sure, no extremely dangerous drugs are sold in this manner: federal regulations see to that. However, there are many drugs that are harmful, and many more that are worthless. One medical authority believes that as many as one-third of all cosmetics, shampoos and deodorants contain potentially harmful ingredients. He expresses the view that this category of products has not been sufficiently checked out by impartial researchers.

"One of the major tasks of consumer protectors in the future," he asserts, "will be the ferreting out of these menaces."

A striking example of a danger area is the cosmetics field. FDA investigators have discovered that many cosmetics contain dangerous quantities of mercury. They fear the consequences for constant users of these products, especially with the creams which may be applied to large areas of the body. Mercury can be absorbed through the skin and stored by the kidneys, where, as it builds up, it can do irreparable damage to these vital organs. In the past, in spite of the fact that the FDA had determined from samples bought at drugstores that many products did contain mercury, it was impossible to force the makers to remove them from the market. The consumer protectors of the FDA had not been given the legal power to treat these toiletries as drugs. Nor could they apply the same standards to them as they did to food. As we have seen in an earlier chapter, the presence of mercury in food is not tolerated except for the minute amount naturally present in tuna fish (.05 parts per million.) Yet mercury in skin-applied substances can just as surely be lodged in the kidneys as mercury ingested in food.

Starting in 1972, some manufacturers recognized the problems and agreed to provide the FDA with lists of ingredients in various products—something they had not done before. Future amendments to food and drug laws promise more powers for the FDA and possibly other agencies, so they can exercise more control over those ingredients whether the companies making the products agree or not.

The need for protection from dangerous substances used in every day products is dramatically and grimly illustrated by the hexachlorophene trouble. This chemical came into wide use in the early 1950s after it was determined by chemical researchers that it had value as an antiseptic. It appeared in mouthwashes, toothpastes, shampoos, deodorants, toilet soap and even in soaps and solutions used in hospitals. Glowing advertisements described its wondrous properties, and the label *Contains Hexachlorophene* became a passport to the saleability of many products.

Then, in the '60s, reports began to pile up showing that, while it might well be a destroyer of certain organisms, unsuspected dangers lurked in the use of hexachlorophene. Chemists had known all along that the substance was a close relative of the herbicides 2,4,5-T and 2,4-D, the notorious defoliants used to sear millions of acres of vegetation in Vietnam. The thought in the mind of Dr. Renate Kimbrough of the U.S. Communicable Disease Center in Atlanta was that this germ-killing chemical, so like the ones which killed plants, might be effective in killing larger organisms. Perhaps it, too, would make a good pesticide. Experiments showed it had deadly powers, all right. It created severe brain damage in rats. Applied to the skin of mice, it sent them into convulsions and death. In other applications to mice and rats, it resulted in the birth of abnormal offspring.

The research in Atlanta formed a link in the chain of evidence that had been developed by the medical profession. One scientific team found that, when used in cosmetics, hexachlorophene could produce skin disorders in the users. This was a relatively minor effect, for in various hospitals it was discovered that babies who mysteriously went into convulsions had been bathed in soap containing as much as 3 per cent hexachlorophene. In other hospitals, where a solution containing the substance had been applied to burn cases, it was discovered that it quickly penetrated the burned skin and entered the blood stream. This discovery lead to other observations and it was soon found that users of soaps and cosmetics containing the substance showed deposits of the chemical in the fatty tissues after just three weeks of ordinary use. It was determined that the larger the area of skin exposed to any product containing hexachlorophene, the greater was the amount of it absorbed into the blood stream. Efforts to wash or rinse it off the skin did not succeed. Some of the substance was left, even after the skin was rinsed with alcohol.

With the dangers of hexachlorophene exposed, it has been abandoned in the products where it proved most menacing. However, there may be many other chemicals used in various common drugstore items that can present dangers. Fortunately, an increasing number of companies are abandoning the "consumer-be-damned" attitude they had in the past. And it may be that as they cooperate with the FDA, the Public Health Service and the medical profession, the potential for drug disasters will be reduced.

"It probably will never be eliminated," says a spokesman for the FDA, who adds:

> The task of protecting the consumer from dangerous and useless drugs is never ending. It's always going to remain one of the greatest challenges for anyone engaged in any phase of consumer protection. There are literally tens of thousands of as yet untried chemicals—and there's no reason to suppose that the effort to use them to save lives and provide better health is going to stop. What we can hope is that the mistakes made in the efforts to apply them won't be allowed to hurt the consumer. It's the job of our scientists to see that they are not.

4. Protecting the Consumer's Money

Protecting the health and safety of consumers may seem more dramatic, but protecting the consumer's money is no less demanding a task. The assault on their pocketbooks is so massive and varied that each year American consumers are being robbed of billions of dollars. Some estimates put a price tag as high as $25,000,000,000 a year on tribute paid to those segments of society that prey on consumers rather than serve them.

What has been called "the great consumer robbery" takes three basic forms:

Defective products and workmanship: Appliances that don't work, houses that fall apart, automobiles that crumple, repairs that don't repair.

Price juggling: Overcharges for goods and services often so cleverly concealed that the consumer doesn't know he's being robbed.

Fraud: The operation of various illegal or barely legal schemes carried out by criminals, or near criminals, to swindle poor and middle-income consumers.

The Quality Problem

The biggest unnecessary grab from the consumer's money is the payment for purchase and upkeep of faulty products. Clothing that rips out at the seams because poor quality thread is used; fabrics that shrink; cleaning compounds that don't clean; clothespins that don't pin—the list is about as long as the list of products our technology spews out in such abundance. However, the greatest losses to consumers occur in the matter of appliances, automobiles and housing—the largest purchases consumers make.

The charges against poorly made appliances can be levied against any of the host of electrically operated devices that abound in the American home. Toasters, mixers, vacuum cleaners, broiler ovens, ranges, washers, dryers, dishwashers, refrigerators, freezers, air conditioners—complaints pile up against them all. Poor design, faulty parts, frequent breakdowns, warranties that do not guarantee anything and leave the consumer to foot the bills—all this is a refrain that runs through the thousands of protests that are filed with consumer protection organizations (and, of course, with manufacturers).

Typical complaints noted by the Office of Consumer Affairs include:

> An air conditioner on which the compressor burned out three times in six months of use.
>
> A dishwasher so badly designed that water hit the motor, soaking it, and causing the motor to burn out repeatedly.
>
> A refrigerator that "sweated" inside, soaking the contents of the refrigerator. The defect could only be corrected by the installation of an additional heater—at the customer's expense.

These are complaints made about expensive, first-line, nationally advertised makes. Moreover, the appliances were not just occasional lemons, because the same difficulties occurred in other appliances of the same make. The defects were "designed in." It is this aspect of the great appliance breakdown that consumer organizations are most hopeful of doing something about. They believe that it is not necessary to build in defects that will create problems for the consumer. A firm resolution to put consumer interests first—ahead of the sales or production interests of the manufacturer—could end much of the trouble.

Many of the breakdowns in appliances can be attributed, not to a callous, don't-give-a-damn attitude on the part of manufacturers, but simply to the increasing complexity of modern appliances. Consider, for example, the refrigerator. Once a compressor and a door switch that operated the light were about the only mechanisms in it. Today a refrigerator may have dozens of operating components. One deluxe model boasts of no less than sixty-three operating parts, including two relays, three solenoids, five thermostats, six motors, eleven switches and twelve heaters—not to mention the basic compressor and the light switch in the door that its primitive ancestor had.

"We *can* make them better," admitted an appliance company engineer to an investigator for a state consumer protection bureau. "It's just a matter of deciding to do so."

He cited the case of a plastic part in a washer that cost 10 cents less than a metal part—and wore out twice as fast. A saving of cents for the manufacturer increased the number of service calls connected with that particular part—all of them occurring *after* the warranty had run out. The company saved $100,000 on one million units—but consumers paid out at least twice that amount on needless service calls. "A simple decision not to save the 10 cents could have given the consumer a much better product."

Rarely, of course, is the matter quite as simple as the example above. The increase in cost required to make a product really as good as it could be might run into several dollars instead of a few cents. However, a consulting engineer for an appliance company anxious to improve its consumer image found out that an average cost of $5 per unit would eliminate three service calls in a five-year period. Marketing surveys showed that the customer would willingly have paid extra for the better machine—as indeed customers do for one famous make washer which consistently costs from $25 to $100 more than competitive makes and which lasts far longer, with almost no service calls.

A frequent complaint made by purchasers of breakdown-prone appliances is that even though these breakdowns occur during the period covered by a warranty, it is hard to get dealers to live up to guarantees. The customer buys a product confident he has a firm guarantee, but down in the fine print are jokers that make him pay for repairs he thought were covered. The Office of Consumer Affairs outlines some of these trick clauses that hurt consumers:

1. The company shall not be responsible for labor and transportation charges incident to replacement of defective parts.
2. This warranty is terminated by removal of the appliance from the premises of original installation.
3. This warranty is effective only while the appliance is used in a private dwelling by the original purchaser only for normal family use.
4. This warranty does not apply to:
   a. Breakage or failure of light bulbs.

    b. Fuses, parts and accessories with porcelain finish or made of glass, filters, gaskets, rubber, and plastic parts.

    c. Loss of refrigerant or replacement of refrigerant.

    d. Incidental or consequential damage.

5. This warranty shall not apply if the original model and serial number plate has been altered, defaced, or removed.

6. This warranty shall be void after eighteen months from date of manufacture, regardless of the installation date.

Pity the poor appliance purchaser who, when he tries to get service, discovers that the dealer has gone out of business or dropped the line. He's in for the warranty runaround, as the new dealer to whom he is referred by the manufacturer refuses to give service on an appliance he didn't sell. One customer with a broken refrigerator was sent to three different dealers after he found the original seller no longer handled the particular make he owned. All three refused to take on the job, and the customer ended up going back to the seller and paying for the servicing—a $95 repair bill—although the warranty was still in full effect. Another customer who had purchased an expensive color TV set that never worked properly found himself unable to get any satisfaction from the selling dealer. Eventually, after repeated complaints, a factory representative came around. He reported that while it was true the set hadn't ever been any good, it was now completely worn out, and in any case the warranty no longer applied.

Consumer organizations are convinced that design could help the warranty problem. By simply making repairs easier to make, the reluctance of dealers could be overcome and the factory could afford to offer more solid guarantees. The goal should be "do-it-yourself" removal units so that either the consumer can simply take a part down to the dealer or store for replacement, or the service man who calls at the home can replace defective parts quickly.

This goal, which presents a ringing challenge to tomorrow's mechanical and electrical engineers, has already been achieved in certain makes of TV sets. A major appliance dealer saw the light as early as 1972 and came up with a line of appliances called "Lifelong." These include a toaster, oven, vacuum cleaner, electric steam iron and an electric coffee maker. They are made so that various parts of these appliances that wear out or go bad can simply be removed by the user and a new component snapped into place.

Many consumer-conscious industrial designers believe that a revolution in simplified appliances must come from the manufacturers. One of them, Jay Dublin, a noted designer, visualizes sturdier as well as simpler appliances having multiple functions. "There are too many separate appliances in the home," he says. "What it leads to is chaos, product pollution. This throws a burden on the housewife that is intolerable. She really doesn't know how to store them, use them, repair them. . . . The products are ill designed for each other. Many of them are parasitic, requiring as much work to get out, put together, use and clean up as did the hand methods they replaced."

The faulty-product problem is overwhelming when it comes to automobiles. Each year Americans spend approximately $30,000,000,000 on automobile repairs. Studies indicate that as much as one-third of that— $10,000,000,000—is thrown away. It goes in payments to crooked and incompetent mechanics. Much of this needless expense to consumers is paid out to correct defects in cars that shouldn't have been there when the new car was delivered to the customer. Consumers Union regularly reports from ten to forty things wrong with each new car it tests. Purchasers who file complaints with consumer organizations sometimes find even more. One irate purchaser of a car for which he paid $5,600 reported no less than fifty-two defects. Poorly put together bodies that let in the rain, loose bolts, leaky hoses, inoperative windshield wipers and faulty heaters are just a few of the common complaints.

These "minor" defects are generally a product of slapdash workmanship and lack of proper inspection at the factory. Researchers report that only about one-tenth of

81

one per cent of the components of a new car are ever inspected. The shiny new automobile that rolls off the assembly line is supposed to be inspected, and anything that didn't get taken care of on the line is supposed to be corrected. However, an inspector for one plant testified before a Senate committee that often "okay stickers" were slapped on cars with known defects.

Such flaws in workmanship are mere annoyances compared to the "designed-in" defects that seriously affect the operation and safety of the car. Faults in design rather than the lack of inspection account for most of the mechanical problems that have caused the recall of millions of cars. A catalog of the reasons why cars have been recalled includes just about every vital part and system of the automobile—steering, brakes, suspension, transmission, engines and electrical wiring. Ralph Nader brought to the attention of a horrified motoring public that motorists were often driving around for years with dangerously defective parts in their cars. A study made for the National Highway Safety Bureau of new cars with 500 or fewer miles showed that 43.9 per cent had one or more potentially dangerous defects.

Car purchasers have assumed that the warranties on their new cars made the manufacturer responsible for correcting defects. They commonly find out something quite different when they take their cars in to the dealers for servicing under the warranty. The warranty customers are the stepchildren of the auto-repair business, often finding it a struggle to get dealers to fix the trouble. The amount of money the dealer gets from the manufacturer is less than the payments he can extract from the customer whose warranty has expired. Therefore, the owner of the new car who takes it to the dealer often finds himself given what is known in the trade as the "sunbath" or the "wall job" treatment. This means that his car is placed out on the lot someplace, or in a remote corner against a wall. When the owner comes back to get it, he learns that the shop has been "too busy" to get to his car. Often, faced with a long wait, the owner will do what the dealer hopes he will do—he goes away. Perhaps he comes back at a later date and finds himself subjected to the same treatment. Many car purchasers have reported as many as ten trips to the dealer—only to end up totally frustrated on getting all the defects corrected. Thousands of car owners have given up in disgust, finally going to other garages where they had to pay for the services required.

One faulty part on modern automobiles has cost motorists a fortune. This is the bumper—a device that is supposed to save a car from damage. Actually, on most cars, the bumper long ago ceased to serve that purpose, becoming instead, with all its glittering chrome, a useless ornament. At one time, bumpers were placed from eight to twelve inches out from body parts. On recent cars, they have been snuggled in against vulnerable sheet metal. Just how vulnerable is this metal is shown dramatically by crash tests carried out by the Highway Safety Commission. In a ten-mile-per-hour-front-and-side crash, a full-sized, 1972-model sedan sustained damage worth $719.25; another ran up a bill of $556.08. The "improved" bumpers on 1973 cars did no better. In fact, they were much worse on some cars, which sustained as much as $1,200 in damages from such crashes. Damages done by a 2.5 mph rear-barrier crash—in which cars were backed into a wall at the sedate speed of a slow-walking pedestrian—ran as high as $112.

"Detroit has to completely revise its thinking about bumpers," says a spokesman for the Insurance Institute of Highway Safety. "There's no good reason why we can't have a bumper that will take up all the shock of low-speed crashes."

Design change is the key challenge to automobile engineers of the future. With the basic price of cars rising every year, one way to give the consumer a break is to find ways to cut the staggeringly high repair bills. In an admonishment to the car makers, a study made by the Department of Transportation says, "It requires increased awareness of maintenance and repair problems at the design stage." Such an awareness, says the study, could save American automobile owners $3,000,000,000 a year!

The quality of newly built houses is another area where consumers have been trampled on. The number of new homes being purchased in the United States is increasing at a fantastic rate. The number of complaints people have about their new homes is increasing even faster.

"Houses just aren't built like they used to be," says an Atlanta building inspector. "Poor materials and workmanship are showing up more and more."

"I really believe the materials in the $28,000 house I bought are substandard," writes one disgruntled homeowner, whose complaints are typical of the thousands of letters received by government consumer agencies. "No room is finished perfectly. We can see daylight in the basement. The kitchen cabinets are coming apart; the house is really falling to pieces. Our glass shower door just exploded one morning, sending glass onto our bed twenty-five feet away."

A New York carpenter concurs with disgruntled homeowners. "Because of the housing conditions in this country today, you've got to produce housing—and produce it fast," he says. "You don't have time to take pride in your work. In one house I was in today, the molding on a kitchen cabinet was one inch out of level. If I had to sit in that kitchen and look at it, I'd get sick. Today builders just don't care. Craftsmen now adopt the attitude that 'I'm not buying this house; I'm just putting it together.'"

"Everybody in our subdivision has had problems," reports a Houston bookkeeper who bought a $30,000 home. "At least four houses have had fires, and we suspect that faulty wiring was the cause. Something is wrong with *all* our wiring. We're always blowing fuses."

In Los Angeles, the roof of a new forty-unit apartment building was leaking before it was six months old. Tenants on the top floor had to be moved out. Repairs were made, but the patch job was ineffective. The building was subsequently sold, leaving the new landlord with the same old leaky roof.

Letters to the President's Office of Consumer Affairs echo consumer complaints heard all over the country. "Paint on the outside woodwork of our home peeled after only four months," wrote one Pennsylvania man. "Wallpaper inside peeled from moisture caused by heavy rains that penetrated the windows. The builder's machinery broke the cement walkway, and he refused to repair the damage."

"I was standing in our bathroom," wrote one Florida woman, "and the floor suddenly collapsed. There wasn't a single support beneath the tiles! Our plumbing leaks, the basement collects water after a heavy rain, our floors are uneven, our doors are hung improperly and don't close, our fuses are constantly blowing and our paint is beginning to peel. The builder keeps postponing making the necessary repairs, and my warranty is about to run out."

"I paid over $40,000 for my new home," says one Albuquerque man, "and so did the rest of the families on my street. We hadn't been living here a year when we woke up one morning and found large cracks in many of our walls. When we called in a building inspector, he told us that faulty workmanship and poor surveying of the construction site were to blame. We were lucky. We were able to make extensive repairs and stay in our homes. Others simply had to move or risk the roof caving in on them."

How is it possible that poor-quality materials and slipshod workmanship show up so often in homes—not only in those costing $15,000, but in $50,000 ones as well? While it may be true that a large percentage of housing contractors build homes with quality and safety in mind, other less scrupulous builders place profits ahead of quality. Some of these contractors—who range from members of multimillion dollar organizations which build giant developments across the country to small local builders—are constantly seeking ways to "cut corners" in order to realize greater profits. This may take the form of using substandard materials in a foundation, which soon cause it to crack. It may mean improper soil and rock studies of building site areas, resulting in buckling and cracking walls. It may even mean using inadequate wiring in walls, which has caused countless numbers of tragic fires.

Poor craftsmanship and the "it's not my home, so why should I care" attitude of some skilled laborers is one outgrowth of this cutting-corners attitude. When a cost-cutting contractor forces a carpenter to use inferior materials and insists that the job be done quickly at the expense of doing it right, it is difficult for a craftsman to take any pride in his finished work.

However, what about building codes, which dictate the minimum standards of materials and workmanship that must go into a home? Originally building codes were written to insure the homeowner that high-quality materials and craftsmanship had gone into the construction of his home. But building codes are effective only when they are enforced by building inspectors. Unfortunately, so many houses are being built in this country that building inspectors' caseloads are extremely high. Inspectors are often so overburdened that they simply cannot devote enough time to any given job. In addition, a good deal of connivance and bribery is possible between builders and inspectors. In the building industry, the old adage "you scratch my back; I'll scratch yours" all too often means I can arrange a better job for you with our firm."

Even federal building codes are difficult to enforce. The Federal Housing Administration is supposed to set construction standards and inspect for compliance before loans are made to home builders. "These 'minimum-property standards,'" reports Ralph Nader, "are taken from industry-developed codes which are full of escape hatches. The FHA's system of home inspection and enforcement to compel the builder to bring housing up to minimum standards is shorthanded, dilatory and sometimes corrupted."

In the past, consumers had little or no recourse when they found that the homes they had purchased were poorly constructed. Complaints made to builders were often ignored. Secure in their knowledge that the purchasers were, more than likely, merely one-time customers, builders did not feel it was necessary to strive to please. Consumers had no one to whom they could turn.

Do we have to accept low standards of housing? Nader and other consumer representatives answer this question with a resounding "no." They tell us that home buyers can and must be an effective force in helping to create good-quality housing. But to accomplish this they will have to play a much larger role than they have in the past in seeing to it that complaints about poor housing do not merely fall on the deaf ears of building contractors.

Virginia Knauer, President Nixon's consumer adviser, suggested forming a "housing complaint clearinghouse," to which consumers can write. From the complaints received, consumer representatives could decide where to move against builders or government officials responsible for deficiencies in housing quality. The National Association of Home Builders has also urged its members to set up committees to which both buyers and builders can go when they are unable to reach an agreement on complaints. A group of this type that has already been set up in Maryland reports that most of the cases brought to it have been settled in favor of the consumer.

Perhaps the boldest proposal for the protection of home buyers is that of Ralph Nader and other consumer protectors. They advocate ten- or twenty-year warranties backed by national home manufacturers and builders and insured by the federal government, much as a federal agency insures bank deposits. Such warranties would certainly be far superior to the weak guarantees now offered by some local contractors and builders. The federal warranty would be teamed with a "truth-in-building" law (much like recent "truth-in-advertising" laws) that would require builders to give home buyers accurate assessments of the quality of both materials and workmanship that have gone into a new home.

Congress is reviewing an extensive plan that would create a government corporation to set national performance and specification standards for the building industry. Senator Jacob Javits of New York and Representative William Moorehead of Pennsylvania are spearheading a congressional drive aimed at establishing a National Institute of Building Sciences, which would issue approvals of acceptable building standards, techniques and materials.

In introducing the legislation, Senator Javits aptly pointed out that "the absence of an authoritative national source to advise the housing industry and local authorities as to the latest technological developments in building materials and construction techniques and to propose nationally acceptable standards for local building codes has proven to be a great obstacle to efforts to meet the national housing goal."

The National Institute of Building Sciences would develop and set standards affecting building materials and local building codes. It would also promote tests of new building products and techniques, and it would provide technical services to teach builders the best ways of using them. The institute's board of directors would be composed of from fifteen to twenty-one members appointed by the president with the advice and consent of the Senate. The National Academy of Science and Engineering's Research Council would be called upon to recommend nominees. The board would have members from professional societies, labor unions and cousumer and public interest groups.

The Pricing Problem

When Senator Roman Hruska presided over hearings by the Senate Antitrust and Monopoly Subcommittee of the Judiciary Committee, he made a humorous remark: "I have an idea that maybe this series of hearings is before the wrong subcommittee. We have another committee that deals with organized crime."

His wry comment was a reference to automobile repair charges, but many defenders of consumer interest feel the same observation applies to a lot of other fields. Car repairs, they maintain, are simply a flagrant example of a problem that confronts consumer protectors—how can we make sure that the consumer pays a fair price for the goods and services he buys?

In theory, in our competitive economy the consumer is protected from overcharges. Presumably the buyer of any product or service is free to shop around, and presumably various enterprises competing for his business will keep prices fair in order to attract buyers. This idealized picture does, to be sure, apply in some areas of retailing, but there are many other areas where it does not. Consumer organizations, both governmental and private, are fighting a wide-ranging battle to control at least some of the most outrageous of the overcharges that levy a multi-billion dollar tax on the consumer.

Automobile repair charges, in spite of years of effort by consumer groups and a vast amount of publicity, still deserve to be called "the great highway rip-off." One practice that causes drivers to pay exorbitantly high prices for auto repairs is the custom of "throwing the book" at the customer. Motor companies and other organizations print a set of price schedules in their so-called "flat rate" manuals. The companies have worked out the amount of time a mechanic should take to perform a given job, and they have printed in their manuals what the garage should charge for that particular service. There is some variation in the times given in these manuals, with some indicating that it takes twice as long for a certain operation as others state. But it is generally agreed by all investigators that most of the flat-rate times are grossly exaggerated. As one cynical mechanic explains, "They took the time required by the slowest, most fumble-fingered mechanic they could find, and then doubled or trebled it." This particular mechanic, highly experienced and competent, stated to a consumer organization investigator: "I haven't found a flat-rate job yet that I couldn't do in half the time allowed. A lot of jobs I can do in one-third the time, and I can show you stuff in the book that I can do in one-fourth the time."

The man was not exaggerating. In a letter received by the Federal Office of Consumer Affairs, a motorist reported that he was charged $2.85 for the labor of putting on a battery terminal bolt. The customer timed the mechanic, who put the bolt on in exactly two minutes. That figured out to a wage of $85.50 an hour. The motorist's protests were met with the statement that the flat-rate manual allowed eighteen minutes for that job— and that's what he had been charged for.

"Flat rating" the customer gets particularly expensive when more than one operation on the same section of the car is being performed. For example, two jobs—both of which require removal of the same wheel—if flat rated will include the manual's charge for removing the wheel twice, even though the mechanic only removes the wheel once.

The unwary customer who is quoted a per-hour charge doesn't realize that he is being quoted "book time" rather than clock time.

The use of the flat-rate manuals is defended on the grounds that sometimes the mechanic can run into a tough job that takes longer than the book. The claim is that the customer is protected because he knows exactly what a particular job will cost. However, countless customers lose for every one who benefits.

Finding some fairer way of charging for auto repairs is a prime objective of consumer organizations. "Somehow we've got to find a way to 'beat the book,'" says a California investigator.

Many consumer advocates feel that the most flagrant cases of price gouging have occurred in the field of prescription drugs. Large pharmaceutical firms have long followed the practice of setting extremely high charges for brand-name drugs which they have developed or on which they have exclusive distribution rights. These charges are much higher than those for the generic drug—an identical drug without the brand name.

A U.S. Senate investigator turned up some startling facts about how this works out in practice. One firm, it was reported, "sells the popular hypertension drug, reserpine, to the pharmacist at $39.50 per 1,000 tablets. This firm wanted to go into the New York market, so it offered the same drug to New York City hospitals at $1.10. The price to the pharmacist was 3,500 per cent higher than the price to New York City under competitive bidding. But even by cutting its price from $39.50 to $1.10, the firm did not win the New York City bid. It went to another firm which had bid seventy-two cents."

This is just one example of many in which the price charged the pharmacist—and, of course, that price is passed on to the consumer, plus a profit for the pharmacist—varied by as much as *10,000 per cent* on some drugs. The outcry against high prices on prescription drugs, and federal regulations requiring the prescribing of drugs by their generic names rather than by brand names, have resulted in lower prices on medicines—an example of the benefits of consumer action coupled with government intervention on behalf of the consumer.

The Frauds That Rob Consumers

"Every year it cheats Americans of more than is lost through robbery, burglary, larceny, auto theft, embezzlement and forgery combined." In these words, Senator Warren Magnuson is referring to the price of consumer frauds—illegal schemes that cheat the unwary consumer. This form of thievery exists in many fields— home improvements, automobile and appliance repairs (not just overcharges, but outright criminal acts), real estate and investment.

Better Business Bureaus and governmental consumer protection departments report that home-improvement swindles provide the biggest take for the swindlers who prey on consumers. The Federal Trade Commission estimates that at least $500,000,000 pours into the pockets of these criminals. Other estimates put the figure much higher.

Many of the home-improvement gyps are based on heating-plant replacements. A typical one operates this way: An official-looking man rings the doorbell of a middle-class home and announces that he is a "heating-plant inspector." If the homeowner makes the mistake of letting him in, the "inspector" proceeds to examine the furnace, shakes his head sadly and says the furnace is "leaking" and must be repaired. He knows just the company to seal up the joints and make the furnace safe. They will only charge $25 or $30 for this service.

The next day the furnace men arrive and proceed to take the furnace apart. When it is all disassembled and the parts are lying out on the basement floor, the homeowner is called down and told the bad news. The furnace is beyond repair. It will endanger the occupants of the house. The homeowner signs a contract for a new furnace—one that is sold to him at an exorbitant price and which may turn out to be inferior. Needless to say, there was nothing the matter with the owner's original furnace in the first place.

Even when the product sold meets a legitimate need, the home-improvement swindlers manage to depart with illicit gains. Often the caper starts with an advertisement in the newspaper offering siding, storm windows, add-on rooms or paint jobs at amazingly low prices. In a typical racket, aluminum siding was offered at a price of $500 for a house of a given size. The homeowner who answered the ad was called upon by a salesman who proceeded to explain that the type of siding offered for that money was flimsy and would be readily dented, even by hailstones. He then had a better grade of siding to offer the homeowner. The eventual price turned out to be more than $2,000. In one case, the homeowner who thought he was going to buy a $500 bargain ended up ordering a $4,500 job. Only after the new siding was installed, did the owner discover that it was actually little better than the flimsy kind he had been offered in the first place.

Better Business Bureau records, which abound with rackets, include such cases as that of a blind man who ordered a small repair job done on his home. That is, he thought that was what he was doing. Actually, he signed a contract—which he could not read—authorizing the company to do a much larger job. Neither job was ever completed. The gyp company sold the contract to a finance company which, when the homeowner did not make payments on it, foreclosed on his home. The blind man, in addition to signing the contract he hadn't read, had also signed a deed of trust on his property.

This was an extreme case, but it is a sad fact that there are all too many schemes for getting people to sign contracts that call for extensive home-improvement jobs at exorbitant prices and high rates of interest. In many cases, the work is not completed or even started, or it turns out to be of poor quality.

Along with frauds that rob homeowners of many thousands of dollars and even cause the loss of their homes, investigators are constantly turning up petty rackets. An example of this occurred in a midwestern city where "driveway specialists" would drive up to a home where the driveway was obviously in bad need of repair. An overall-clad workman would ring the doorbell and announce that he and his crew had been installing a driveway at a nearby home. It just so happened that they had a lot of material left over—enough to pave another small driveway like this one. Ordinarily the job would cost $800 but, under the circumstances, they would do it right away for $400. Of course, the homeowner would have to make up his mind at once. Flustered and pressured, with what seemed like a great bargain in sight, he or she would often agree. The men would proceed to put in the asphalt driveway and collect their money. Everything would look satisfactory, for a time. The trouble would come with the first rain, when the thin asphalt coating would wash completely away. Any efforts to find the contractor would be met with failure, because such crews quickly move on to other towns.

Repair rackets involving home appliances do not swindle any one householder quite as much, but they do add up to many hundreds of millions of dollars extracted from consumers' pockets. Consumer organizations do not have any exact figure for this, because most of the depradations of crooked appliance repairmen never come to light. Many incidents are not reported, even when the householder realizes he's been "had." And, in other cases, the luckless owners of broken appliances never find out the truth. Just about every kind of major appliance is subject to racketeering on the part of unscrupulous repairmen. The repairman takes the balky device back to the shop and, regardless of what is wrong with it, finds enough things to run up a bill to whatever size he thinks the particular customer can be taken for.

Color TV sets are probably the most problematical of all appliances, because, although the trouble is likely to be minor, the customer is easily convinced that what's wrong is something major. The state of California, which pioneered a law that has stopped much TV racketeering, has ample evidence of this. The law requires TV, phonograph, tape and radio gear dealers to be licensed in order to do business in the state. If the dealer is caught in any fraudulent repairs, he loses his license and is put out of business. The investigators for the consumer agency that patrols these repairmen has set up an effective system for catching these individuals red-handed. The technique is to place decoy TV sets in private residences. The sets are in perfect working order, except for one defective tube which has been deliberately placed in the set. When a call goes out to a repair shop, about which complaints have been received or which there is reason to suspect skullduggery, the repairman picks up the set. If it is returned with a bill for the standard service call, plus the tube, the shop gets a clean bill of health. If it comes back with a bill for $25, $50, $75—figures that are not uncommon—for mythical repairs, the dealer is obviously guilty of cheating. Conviction on this evidence can result in a penalty of ninety days in jail.

The auto-repair industry, which has accumulated such a bad record of incompetent work and overcharges for its services, also has a black mark for the perpetration of out-and-out frauds. The vast majority of garages, service stations and auto dealers are not actually crooked, but enough of them are to swindle car owners out of possibly half a billion dollars a year. Rackets cover a wide spectrum of crimes. At the petty theft end they include such tricks as the tire-slashing dodge. A customer drives into the service station and, while pretending to inspect a tire, the attendant jabs a sharpened screwdriver into the tire. Then he calls the attention of the motorist to the slashed tire, and quite probably succeeds in convincing him that it is beyond repair, which it may well be. The result is the sale of a new tire at a high price. Another petty service station gag is to twist the windshield wiper out of shape.

Protecting the Consumer's Money

While no one motorist loses much by these minor methods of thievery, an individual car owner can lose hundreds of dollars on major repair rackets. The FTC had to prosecute a transmission franchise outfit for numerous schemes of defrauding customers. One of them was to tear down the transmission of a car brought in for inspection or routine servicing. The customer would then be told that the transmission needed to be replaced —at a cost of $250 or more. To add insult to injury, it was found that in a number of cases the same old transmission had been painted and reinstalled. Similar schemes have been commonly worked by concerns doing engine work.

Way back in 1872 a law against fraud-by-mail was passed. Postal inspectors are still fighting to enforce that law, and subsequently strengthened ones, against hordes of wily operators who try to carry out an amazing number of dirty tricks. The inspectors, in fact, conduct as many as 10,000 investigations a year, with the frauds falling into many categories. Some of the major ones are:

Confidence swindles. Promotional literature claims that the recipient can get rich quick by purchasing exclusive rights to sell certain products in his community. These products include vending machines, lines of cosmetics, toys and power tools. The products are not of the quality claimed, the purchaser of the franchise is required to buy huge quantities of them and it usually turns out that there really is no market for the items.

101

Correspondence schools. Fly-by-night schools offer courses in all kinds of professions, for which the person to whom they sell the course could not possibly qualify. Guarantees of jobs for the persons who sign up for expensive courses are not fulfilled.

Memberships. Pay a $5 to $10 fee and you get to be a "member" of a discount club that will thereafter sell you merchandise at ridiculously low prices. After getting enough members, the club "disappears."

Work-at-home schemes. "You can earn $50 a week addressing envelopes at home in your spare time." Millions of people, many of them handicapped or aged, have sent in the one dollar requested by operators of work-at-home schemes for information about how to get in on this money-making home business. The information is worthless. Another racket is to sell machines that will knit garments, make plastic signs, etc. The law is broken when the company breaks its promise to buy the merchandise turned out by the buyer of the machine—if the merchandise is satisfactory. The company, however, never finds the work acceptable.

The Post Office can cite dozens of other schemes, as well as scores of variations of these. In spite of the diligence of the postal inspectors, these mail gyps continue to extract more than $500,000,000 from American consumers every year.

THE CAREERS

5. On the Firing Line—Careers in Consumer Education, Inspection and Law Enforcement

The growing number of laws and regulations designed to protect the consumer present an exciting career challenge. Making sure that the hard-won battles of the consumer advocates stay won calls for a vast number of inspectors. It calls, too, for other firing-line workers who help the consumer help himself. Their task is consumer education—giving the consumer the advice and information that help him protect his rights.

Home Economists

The influence of the home economist on the consumer's welfare is tremendous. No single professional career offers such a variety of possibilities to anyone who wants to serve the consumer. The old picture of "home economics" as a glorified name for cooking and sewing is out of date today and will be even more out of date in the future. The home economist is concerned with the full range of consumer products—not only to help make them better, but to educate the consumer to use them.

This statement from the Home Economics Education Bureau of the United States Department of Health, Education and Welfare presents an accurate picture of the opportunities in this profession. As one home economics veteran puts it, "You might say we're the original consumer protectors, who are just coming into our own in this new era of concern for consumers."

The influence of the home economist starts in the branch of the profession that still is the major source of employment for home economists—teaching. The courses these home economists teach in high school and college are increasingly termed "consumer education," although, of course, they include more traditional subjects such as food, nutrition, clothing, textiles, child development, family relations, home furnishings and home management. In addition, home economists may sponsor local chapters of Future Homemakers of America and conduct related activities. Teachers in adult education programs help homemakers increase their understanding of family relations and improve their homemaking skills. They also train those who wish to prepare for jobs in home economics. College teachers may combine teaching and research, and often they specialize in one particular area of home economics.

Private business firms and trade associations employ home economists to promote the development, use and care of specific home products. These home economists may do research; test products; prepare advertisements and booklets with instructional materials; plan, prepare and present programs for radio and television; serve as consultants; give lectures and demonstrations before the public; and conduct classes for such workers as salesmen and appliance servicemen.

Home economists employed by food manufacturers often work in test kitchens or laboratories to improve products or help create new products. They may also publicize the nutritional value of specific foods. Those people employed by utility companies describe the operation and benefits of appliances and services and often give advice on household problems. Home economists employed by manufacturers of kitchen and laundry equipment may work with engineers on product development. Those engaged in communications are employed by magazines, newspapers, radio and television stations, advertising and public relations agencies, trade associations and other organizations. They usually prepare articles, advertisements and speeches about home products and services. Their work may include product testing and analysis and the study of consumer-buying habits. Still other home economists work for dress-

107

pattern companies, department stores, interior design studios and other business firms that design, manufacture and sell products for the home. A number of home economists are employed in financial institutions, giving customers advice on spending, saving and budgeting.

Of course, all these activities carried out for private companies are aimed at furthering the business interests of the employers. Yet the home economist in any of these commercial enterprises is increasingly able to play the role of consumer advocate.

"When I went to work for a company making a home appliance, I told them frankly that their product was poorly designed and downgraded by a consumer research organization," explains a home economist who is now a vice president of the company. "They admitted that this was the case, and asked me to join in an effort to develop a better product. The engineers took my advice about a lot of things when they redesigned all the company line. Before, engineers hadn't really consulted with home economists at all—hard as that may be to believe."

Another home economist, working for a small food company, reports:

> One of the products our company was turning out was inferior. However, it was selling well and there had been no complaints. I felt we could improve it greatly. Even if there was no sales reason, we'd be

giving the consumer a better break. In the long run it seemed to me that that was what we had to consider. So I became a sort of consumer spokesman in the company, and they listened to me. Actually, it turned out that, while I was right about the product, I was wrong about the possibility that we could improve it. Eventually it was taken off the market, and another more acceptable item substituted for it in the company's sales offerings.

A home economist working for a utility company worked for consumers in another way. She was able to set up a better system for handling consumer complaints than that worked out by the management.

Examples of such new-found influence on the part of home economists are numerous. Business is definitely listening to the voice of the consumer—and home economists are the ones to help business turn the listening into action.

Home economists are finding ever more important roles in government agencies—state, federal and local—charged with enforcing the laws and regulations that protect the consumer. Product research, testing and consumer education are three broad areas in which home economists serve in these organizations.

An important group of consumers are those on welfare. Here, home economists join with social workers to act as advisers and consultants on household budgets and improved homemaking. They help handicapped

109

homemakers and their families adjust to physical limitations by changing the arrangements in the home and by revising methods of work. Other home economists in welfare agencies supervise or train workers who provide temporary or part-time help to households disrupted by illness.

Approximately 400 colleges and universities offer training leading to a bachelor's degree in home economics, which qualifies graduates for most entry positions in the field. A master's or doctor's degree is required for college teaching, for certain research and supervisory positions, for work as an extension specialist or supervisor and for some jobs in the nutrition field.

The undergraduate curriculum in home economics gives students a strong background in science and liberal arts and also includes courses in each of the areas of home economics. Students majoring in home economics may specialize in various subject-matter areas. Advanced courses in chemistry and nutrition are important for work in foods and nutrition; science and statistics for research work; and journalism for advertising, public relations work and all other work in the communications field. To teach home economics in a high school, a student must complete the professional education courses and other state requirements for a teacher's certificate.

Scholarships, fellowships and assistantships are available for undergraduate and graduate study. Although colleges and universities offer most of these financial grants, government agencies, research foundations, businesses and the American Home Economics Association Foundation provide additional funds.

In federal employment, a home economist's salary starts at $8,055, and with experience it goes up to as high as $17,497 on 1974 salary schedules. In private employment, starting salaries generally run from $9,000 to $25,000, with a few salaries much higher.

Dieticians And Nutritionists

The guardians of an increasingly important area of consumer concern—nutrition—are the professional dieticians. The work of a dietician is traditionally defined as "the planning of nutritious and appetizing meals to help people maintain or recover good health." This is still true, but the fact that the nutritional value of food is just as important as its purity is giving the dietician a greatly widened scope.

A number of federal agencies are working on aspects of nutrition as it concerns the consumer. One consumer protection activity is being carried out by the Food and Drug Administration. It takes the form of requiring nutrition labels on food products. The FDA's slogan "Read the Label—Set a Better Table" is based on the information each label must supply. This includes the size of a serving, the number of servings per container, the number of calories, the protein, carbohydrate and fat content and the percentage of daily requirements of protein, vitamins and minerals the item provides.

Behind the scenes dieticians employed by government agencies and private concerns help check out the information that goes on the labels. Even more important, they are part of the teams seeking to develop products that give consumers more nutrition for the money.

Your work as a dietician would most likely be in one of three fields. You could become an administrative dietician, a therapeutic dietician or a public health nutritionist.

Administrative dieticians apply the principles of nutrition and sound management to large-scale meal planning and preparation, such as that done in hospitals, universities, schools and other institutions. They supervise the preparation of meals; select, train and direct food-service supervisors and workers; arrange for the buying of food, equipment and supplies; enforce sanitary and safety regulations; and prepare records and reports. Dieticians who are directors of a dietary department also formulate departmental policy; coordinate dietary service with the activities of other departments; and are responsible for the development and management of the dietary department budget, which in large organizations may amount to millions of dollars annually.

Therapeutic dieticians plan and supervise the service of meals to meet the nutritional needs of patients. They discuss food likes and dislikes with patients and note

Engineers help auto companies pay more attention to consumer needs. Here retractable rulers determine the comfortable reaching distance to thirty-five different locations on an instrument panel. *General Motors*

Roadside tests of automobiles to check the condition of emission controls and other equipment will become a familiar part of consumer protection efforts in the future. *Traveller's Research Corp.*

Biologists keep close check on pesticide residues in their efforts to keep dangerous chemicals from showing up in the foods we eat. *U. S. Soil Conservation Service*

Meat inspection procedures begin in the stockyards. *USDA*

Home economists are key workers in consumer protection. They evaluate products and advise consumers on how to use them. *SBA Photo Service*

Is the consumer getting the food he pays for? Government and industry inspectors keep close tabs on weighing machines. *Corn Products Co.*

Food inspectors save lives by making sure harmful organisms do not get into food products. *Bureau of Commercial Fisheries*

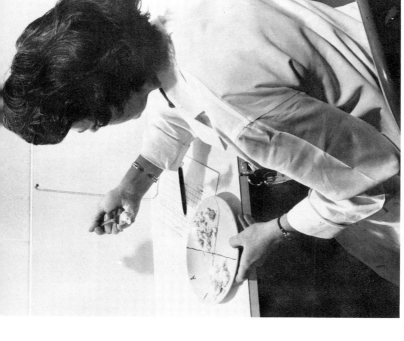

Taste, nutritional value and purity of foods are all concerns of professional dieticians. *U. S. Atomic Energy Commission*

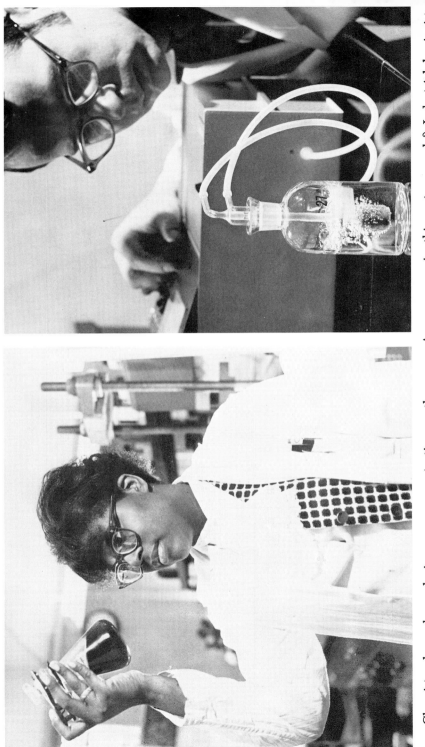

Chemists play a key role in consumer protection as they test and analyze many products. *SBA Photo Service*

Any mercury in this water sample? Industrial hygienists are responsible not only for the well-being of employees but for the safety of products produced by the plant. *Calgon*

The design of safe toys for children is one of the most
rewarding challenges for engineers. *Western Electric*

Designers and engineers work to make home products safer. Plastic bottles have prevented many injuries. *Goodyear News Bureau*

Better materials for homes will come from tests revealing the durability of different chemical treatments for wood. *U. S. Forest Products Laboratory*

Test engineers deliberately set fires to find out ways to make homes more fireproof. *Underwriter's Labs*

their intake of food. Other duties of therapeutic dieticians include calculating modified diets, conferring with doctors regarding patients' diets, instructing patients and their families on the requirements and importance of their diets and suggesting ways to help them stay on these diets after leaving the hospital. In a small institution, one person may serve as both the administrative and therapeutic dietician.

As a public health nutritionist, you would be employed by a public health or welfare agency of the state, county or city. You would work out the nutritional needs of infants, children, mothers, the chronically ill, the disabled and the aging.

The minimum educational requirement for dieticians is a bachelor's degree with a major in foods and nutrition or institution management. This degree can be obtained in about 400 colleges and universities. Undergraduate work should include courses in foods and nutrition, institution management, chemistry, bacteriology and physiology and such related courses as mathematics, psychology, sociology and economics.

To qualify for professional recognition, The American Dietetic Association recommends after graduation the completion of internship programs or two years of preplanned experience. The programs and experience must be approved by the association. Many employers prefer to hire dieticians who have completed an internship. An important phase of the intern's education is clinical experience; the remainder of the internship is devoted to classroom study of menu planning, budgeting, management, other advanced subjects and special projects. Students in a few schools can complete a coordinated education program, also approved by the association, which qualifies them to practice immediately after graduation and without further internship.

Dieticians can expect to start at salaries of around $8,000 in governmental positions and $9,000 in private organizations. Earnings in government are $17,500 tops, but go up to $25,000 in private employment.

Food Inspectors

Floodwaters roar through a midwestern city, damaging a quantity of packaged food in a flooded warehouse. Is it fit for human consumption? The water has hardly receded before a federal food inspector appears to examine the water-soaked packages.

Are the conditions in the kitchen of a restaurant in keeping with the elegance of its dining room? A food inspector takes his place beside the chef to find out.

Do foods produced by a canning factory deserve to carry a United States Department of Agriculture label indicating their quality? A food inspector stands guard to make sure that they do.

The work of food inspectors who enforce the many laws that protect food varies, depending on the particular federal, state or local agency they work for. Some are concerned only with food quality—not its purity. Others are concerned with the purity of a variety of foods. Still others are specialists responsible for only one kind of food, such as meat. Some range over a large area, checking food in many plants and institutions. Others are assigned to one food-processing plant. Some have outdoor jobs; others work inside the year round. Some work in rural areas, others in the heart of big cities. Some are food technologists or food scientists; others are drawn from a variety of scientific, technical and agricultural backgrounds. They all have a common purpose, however, and, indeed, often work together as teams in their efforts to protect the food supply of the American consumer.

Public Health Inspectors. Perhaps the most familiar inspectors in the public health field are the municipal and county employees who inspect food serving establishments. In most communities, restaurants are given sanitation ratings, which you have probably noticed posted in prominent places in various restaurants. The A, B or C rating that is commonplace refers not to the excellence of the cuisine, but to the degree with which the establishment observes the rules that keep the food served safe to eat. Inspectors have an exact guide as to just what to look for in the recommendations of the United States Public Health Service known as the "Mode Ordinance and Code for Food Service Sanitation, 1962." In it the USPHS has set up a model ordinance which has been adopted by most communities in the nation. It provides that "at least once every six months the health authority shall inspect each food serving establishment."

An important part of the duties of the inspectors is the education of the people who work in restaurants. This is no easy task, because the turnover among the nearly 1,500,000 workers in restaurants and other food-serving establishments is high—about 40 per cent a year. Many public health departments have set up programmed learning courses which teach the personnel elementary principles of sanitation.

Most public health inspectors work at the production end of food. An example is their inspection of milk, which they follow from the milking barn to the tank trucks that transport it to the creameries that process and package it. They are constantly engaged in taking samples which are analyzed in state laboratories or sent to two great research institutions maintained by the USPHS—the Robert A. Taft Sanitary Engineering Laboratory in Cincinnati and the Communicable Disease Center in Atlanta. Inspectors for the various government agencies not only work closely with each other, but also with their counterparts in private industry, such as the big milk cooperatives which control much of the milk production in the country.

FDA Inspectors. Milk and shellfish are the particular province of the USPHS. The federal agency concerned with the purity of a wide variety of foods is the Food and Drug Administration. Its inspectors, says an FDA report,

> carry on periodic inspections of food plants and warehouses. They examine and collect samples of food commodities prior to shipment in interstate commerce, during interstate shipment, and while the commodities are being held for sale following shipment.
>
> These men carry out thousands of inspections each year in establishments ranging from bakeries doing a small amount of interstate business, to canneries making shipments to all parts of the United States. Their scene of activities may vary from a cabbage field to the office of the president of a large food corporation.
>
> Other specially trained FDA inspectors examine and collect samples of products which have been offered for importation into the United States.
>
> Scientists in each FDA district laboratory have electronic equipment capable of conducting the most sophisticated types of food analyses.
>
> From the observations of the inspector and the analytical results obtained on any sample collected,

CAREERS IN CONSUMER PROTECTION

a picture of compliance or of noncompliance is drawn.

Observations of the inspector may result in nothing more than a few suggestions on how the manufacturer can improve the sanitary safeguards in his operation.

On occasion, however, the inspector's report coupled with laboratory examination may show a picture of extremely poor manufacturing practices which result in adulterated food products.

Then it becomes necessary to track down the food lots suspected of being contaminated and to take appropriate regulatory action.

With many thousands of manufacturers, distributors, and storers of foods, drugs, therapeutic devices, and cosmetics carrying on business which has a substantial effect on interstate commerce, each district office must carefully program its plans for regulatory checking.

This has led to installation in district offices of an automated system to handle the district's inventory of regulated industries.

Each district is assigned quotas for sampling and inspection in such food projects as grains, dairy products, beverages, bakery goods, fish, fruits, and other commodities.

The districts have considerable autonomy in programming the assignments necessary to fill quotas. This helps avoid inspectional gaps in the coverage of the regulated industries over an area which may include several states.

Each district office and resident inspection station keeps in close contact with the state health and regulatory officials.

It is not unusual for a food plant to receive an unannounced visit from an inspection team made up of state and FDA personnel. State officials have used their special embargo powers against goods found contaminated during such inspections.

Grading Specialists. Little known to the general public is the form of consumer protection that has a profound effect on the quality of the food that reaches supermarket shelves and produce counters. The grading program of the USDA's Consumer and Marketing Service is designed to establish and maintain standards that enable the consumer to judge the quality of food. These standards are reflected in labels which you may have noticed on various food products:

PACKED UNDER CONTINUOUS INSPECTION OF THE U.S. DEPARTMENT OF AGRICULTURE

U.S. GRADE AA WHEN GRADED PACKED UNDER THE SUPERVISION OF THE USDA

OFFICIALLY GRADED

The inspectors who have the job of grading and assigning labels to food products are employed by the

119

USDA, which contracts with the individual company to grade its products. Before the USDA will start a continuous inspection program, a survey inspection of the plant is made to determine whether the plant and methods operation are adequate and suitable. The buildings and the equipment must be properly constructed and maintained in a sanitary condition.

After a plant is approved for continuous inspection, one or more inspectors are assigned to be present at all times when the plant is operating to make continuous in-process checks on the preparation, processing and packing operations. Each inspector makes out a daily quality report on the grade of all products going through the plant. He also makes a continuing check on the general operating conditions of the plant. On the basis of these expert reports, the plant management can control any problems before they become serious and can take the necessary steps to keep the right to the quality labels.

Many food companies which do not contract with the USDA for its service have their own graders and quality inspectors. Their work does not, of course, earn the company the right to use the grade label, but in many cases the standards of quality are as high as those enforced by the USDA. The work of a grading specialist for a private company is of the same general nature and requires the same skills and knowledge of food products as does that of the USDA employee carrying out this important phase of consumer protection.

Meat Inspectors. A career opportunity in consumer protection is service in the meat inspection program of the United States Department of Agriculture and in state agencies. This work is carried out by professional veterinarians charged with the task of assuring the purity and wholesomeness of all meat and poultry which reaches the American consumer.

Inspection begins in the stockyards before the animals are driven in for slaughter or, in the case of poultry, on the trucks as the birds arrive at the processing plant. Any animal that looks abnormal in any way is tagged. It may be either with *U.S. Condemned* or *U.S. Suspect*, depending on how serious the condition appears. This tag has a serial number for follow-through identification. An animal tagged as condemned is disposed of under supervision to prevent contamination of healthy, wholesome meat. An animal that is questionable is also kept apart and is slaughtered separately. Only animals and birds which appear completely healthy are sent along for normal slaughter. After slaughter, guided by detailed regulations, the inspector examines the carcass by sight, incision, touch and smell. He checks for any condition that would indicate unfitness of the carcass for use as human food.

Every container bearing a poultry carcass is identified

121

as INSPECTED FOR WHOLESOMENESS BY THE U.S. DEPARTMENT OF AGRICULTURE. Each animal carcass found free from diseases or objectionable conditions is marked U.S. INSPD & PSD. Every important cut of meat is then marked with the federal meat inspection stamp.

The inspection of meats includes those imported into the United States. USDA inspectors are stationed at strategic locations throughout the country. They inspect each shipment of meat and poultry products, and they double check by submission of samples to a USDA lab. Once imported meat or poultry is okayed by the inspectors, it is treated as a federally inspected product. This inspection on entry is simply the final stage of an inspection system that extends to the country from which the meat came. United States regulations made under the Imported Meat Act and the Poultry Products Inspection Act require that no meat or meat products may enter this country unless they have been prepared under an official national system of inspection substantially equivalent to that of the United States. Before any foreign meat or poultry is approved, the regulations in the foreign country are carefully reviewed. Veterinarian meat inspectors from the United States travel to the foreign country and make extensive inspections in the plants from which the imported meat will come. From time to time, follow-up inspections are made in foreign plants.

Educational Requirements For Food Inspectors. Most food inspectors are drawn from the scientific disciplines (see Chapter 6)—chiefly food science, food technology and various life sciences. Some are also engineers, industrial hygienists and chemists. Most inspection careers are open only to college graduates, usually those with an advanced degree. However, some are open to technicians who have taken a suitable training course (see Chapter 8).

A career as a USDA meat inspector has special requirements, since it calls for a degree as a veterinarian. Meat and poultry inspection services maintained by states for products that do not enter interstate commerce have similar requirements. However, in both services, some technician grade inspectors may serve as assistants to the full inspectors who do have degrees as veterinarians.

Minimum requirements for the D.V.M. or V.M.D. degree are two years of pre-veterinary college work followed by four years of study in a college of veterinary medicine. However, most candidates complete three or four years of a pre-veterinary curriculum (emphasizing the physical and biological sciences). Veterinary college training includes considerable practical experience diagnosing and treating animal diseases and performing surgery and laboratory work in anatomy, biochemistry and other scientific and medical subjects.

There were eighteen colleges of veterinary medicine

123

in the United States in 1970. Some of the qualifications considered by these colleges in selecting students are scholastic record, amount and character of pre-veterinary training, health and an understanding and affection for animals. Since veterinary colleges are largely state supported, residents of the state in which the college is located usually are given preference. In the South and West, regional educational plans permit cooperating states without veterinary schools to send a few students to designated regional schools. In other areas, colleges that accept a certain number of students from other states usually give priority to applicants from nearby states without veterinary schools. The number of women students in veterinary colleges is relatively small; about 9 per cent of the students in 1970 were women.

Needy students may obtain loans and scholarships of up to $2,500 a year to pursue full-time study leading to the degree of Doctor of Veterinary Medicine, under provisions of the Veterinary Medical Education Act of 1966 and the Health Manpower Act of 1968. The United States Department of Agriculture offers students who have completed their junior year in schools of veterinary medicine opportunities to serve as trainees during the summer months.

Investigators And Consumer Counselors

Your career as a consumer protector may be one of a whole new range of occupations concerned with offering advice to consumers and unmasking frauds that bilk consumers of their money. Practitioners of these new professions, as they are taking shape in the mid-1970s, are drawn from many backgrounds. A 1974 survey of government and private consumer-protection organizations showed just how wide an occupational spectrum these new careers covered. Workers included accountants, teachers, engineers, journalists, lawyers, social workers and private detectives.

The organizations for which these people work include state, county and city consumer protection agencies set up to give consumers advice about their rights, to investigate consumer complaints and to bring legal action against consumer exploiters.

Independent consumer-interest organizations conduct investigations, publish reports and serve their membership in various ways.

Business-maintained organizations are devoted to making business more responsive to consumer needs. The Better Business Bureaus and some trade associations and cooperatives are in this category.

Federal agencies, such as the Office of Consumer Affairs, the Product Safety Commission, the Federal Trade Commission and the Postal Service, are charged with protecting various phases of consumer interest.

Private concerns with consumer-relations departments deal with consumer complaints.

Consumer counselors work directly with consumers, making sure they get what they pay for. The three phases of consumer counseling work—receiving complaints, investigating them and helping to reach a settlement of them—all require a knowledge of human nature as well as of products and services, for a large part of the work of consumer investigator-counselors involves talking to people persuasively.

A glance at these three areas of activity will give you a hint of their exciting challenge:

Receiving complaints. Many consumer complaints are received by mail. A California agency, receiving a total of 50,000 complaints, reports that about one-third were received by mail. A large number of consumer complaints come in by telephone. "I spend most of my day on the phone," says a Pennsylvania consumer agency worker. "It often takes half an hour to get all the facts about a consumer complaint." Better Business Bureaus all over the country have discovered that it is hard to keep up with the flood of telephoned complaints. In fact, they get many complaints about *that*—callers object to finding the lines busy. BBB offices are constantly installing more telephones after discovering that the lines at some were busy 50 per cent of the time.

An increasing number of complaints will be delivered in person. "It's the best way," says the head of a busy Chicago consumer-membership organization, "but it's the most time consuming. We're going to need a vast increase in manpower if we hope to really serve the great number of consumers."

Better Business Bureaus are in the forefront of an

effort to make it easier for consumers to register their complaints by sitting down across the desk from a counselor. In a number of cities, the BBB has put mobile units into the field—trucks converted into offices. These traveling offices have been particularly active in poorer sections of the city among groups most often victimized by various kinds of frauds. The strategy of some state agencies is to open "store-front offices." A future development may be the opening of such offices in major shopping centers as well as in downtown areas.

Investigation. Checking out the complaints may be simply a matter of discussions with the offending business firm. It may involve fieldwork, consisting of going to the complainant's home and to the offices or plant of the business firm. One investigator for a voluntary consumer organization in New York broke up a widespread fraud involving the sale of aluminum siding. Acting as an undercover agent, the investigator applied for a job as a salesman for the fraudulent firm. The instructions he received from company officials provided the evidence against the firm that brought to a halt the procedures that were getting unwary consumers to sign contracts involving prices ten times those quoted in company advertisements.

Settlement. Getting the consumer's money back, or having the unsatisfactory product or service replaced with a satisfactory one, is the final challenge to the consumer counselor.

"If we don't get a proper settlement, receiving the

complaint and getting the goods on a company don't mean much," comments a San Francisco consumer counselor. "Fortunately, that is not too hard to do when you're dealing with a company that wants to stay in business. The fly-by-night ones—well, that's a different story."

The Better Business Bureaus have set up a procedure for dealing with complaints that serves as a blueprint for other organizations. This is a system of arbitration, in which the customer's complaint and the business firm's side of the story are referred to an impartial arbitrator, who may be a technical expert in the field, a lawyer or an informed layman. The BBB system is an alternative to legal action, which can be long and costly and which doesn't always help the consumer.

"Actually, when we get a case worked up to the point of arbitration," says a BBB counselor, "it's as good as decided in favor of the consumer—with no trouble to him." In Albuquerque, for example, a batch of 500 cases was brought up to the arbitration stage. In 486 of these cases the accused firm settled before the case went to the arbitrator.

"As we make progress in putting the perpetrators of actual criminal frauds out of business," says a spokesman for the national headquarters of the BBB,

> our organizations, and other consumer-aiding organizations, will be performing the biggest service for

the consumer in this area. After all, it's not much satisfaction for a consumer to know that a fraudulent firm has been put out of business if he—the consumer—is left holding the bag. Therefore I think that anyone entering this field should think of himself or herself not as some sort of criminal prosecutor of scoundrels, but as a friend of both consumer and business. The best hope for the consumer is certainly to reach the point where it is recognized that what's best for the consumer is best for business. That may be a pretty idealistic goal, but it's one that anyone engaged in consumer protection work would do well to hope and work for.

In all three of these aspects of investigation and counseling work in a consumer-protection organization, there is, of course, much variation from one organization to another. An employee of a Better Business Bureau will not be dealing with the same kind of complaints or handling them in the same way as will a person working for a consumer-membership organization. An employee of a federal agency—for instance, a postal inspector—will certainly not be carrying out his duties in the same manner as will a person working for a municipally maintained agency. Nor will earnings and other conditions of employment be the same. In fact, it is hard to give more than a broad range of salaries in this field. It may be stated, however, that the earning potential runs from $8,000 to $26,000—the top figure being the highest salary paid postal inspectors. In private industry, in the case of an executive assigned to consumer relations, the salary range will be that of other executives in the company, which may run $50,000 or more.

The career opportunities in this field do have one factor in common. They are not really open to beginners in any profession. Almost all persons drawn into the field are college graduates who have already had considerable experience in other fields. "It's a sort of graduate level of consumer protection," says a twenty-nine-year-old engineer who became a consumer counselor and investigator after seven years of experience in industrial design. "But it's worth waiting for—and working toward. I don't think there's a more challenging opportunity for anyone who really wants to help the great American consumer."

6. Science Careers in Consumer Protection

A chemist discovers a hazardous chemical in the handle of a toothbrush—mercury—which could be ingested by the user.

A marine biologist notices an organism growing in the polluted water near a shellfishing grounds. He knows that poisons given off by the organism—microscopic plants that flourish in polluted water—will make the shellfish unfit for human consumption.

A physicist checking out an X-ray device used for examining the baggage of airline passengers discovers that harmful radiation is escaping, endangering people exposed to it.

A pathologist examining lab animals that have been given a widely used household remedy learns that they have suffered kidney damage.

These are typical examples of scientists working to advance the cause of consumer protection. They are carrying out the resolution of today's scientists to make science relevant to human needs. Most scientists are not working directly in the field of consumer protection, but more and more of them are finding that their knowledge in both the physical and life sciences can be applied to giving the consumer a better deal than he has had in the past.

If you have been thinking about a career in science and would like to channel it along the lines of consumer protection, the opportunity to do so is wide open. Even a quick glance at some of the possibilities reveals potentials that you may want to explore further.

Life Scientists

Several types of life scientists are concerned with aspects of consumer protection. Their work is primarily in the laboratory, dealing with research and the measurement of the effects of drugs and chemicals.

If you seek a professional career in the life sciences, you should plan on obtaining an advanced degree—preferably a Ph.d. in your chosen field. A bachelor's degree with a major in one of the life sciences will enable you to get a beginning job, but your best chance to advance in your field and get the opportunity to do meaningful work calls for an advanced degree. A Ph.d is an absolute necessity for the higher level research positions in which you might make the greatest contributions to consumer protection. You may, of course, choose to do what many entering the life sciences do—get your bachelor's degree and enter into a period of actual employment before returning to college for your higher degree.

A bachelor's degree will qualify you for positions involving testing and production and operation work, and you will have some duties connected with the enforcement of government regulations. You may also obtain a position as an advanced technician, particularly in the area of medical research.

Training leading to a bachelor's degree with a major in one of the life science specialties is offered by nearly all colleges and universities. Courses differ greatly from one college to another, and it is important that a student determine which college program best fits his or her interests and needs. In general, liberal arts colleges and universities emphasize training in the biological sciences and medical research. State universities and land-grant colleges offer special advantages to those people interested in agricultural sciences, because their agricultural experiment stations provide many opportunities for practical training and research work.

Prospective life scientists should obtain the broadest undergraduate training possible in all branches of biology and in related sciences, particularly biochemistry, organic and inorganic chemistry, physics and mathematics. Courses in statistics, calculus, biometrics and computer programming analysis are becoming increas-

133

ingly essential. Training and practice in laboratory techniques, in the use of laboratory equipment and in fieldwork are also important.

Advanced degrees in the life sciences also are conferred by a large number of colleges and universities. Requirements for advanced degrees usually include fieldwork and laboratory research, as well as classroom studies and preparation of a thesis.

Biochemists have a unique role in the realm of science, for they work in both the life sciences and the physical sciences, combining biology and chemistry. A biochemist's work is sometimes described as dealing with "living chemistry"—the study of the chemistry of living organisms. The field of biochemistry is an increasingly important one in the broad area of consumer protection. Biochemists identify and analyze the chemical processes related to biological functions, such as muscular contraction, reproduction and metabolism. This gives them the basic knowledge necessary to investigate the effects on organisms of such chemical substances as foods, hormones and drugs.

Biochemists study a wide variety of substances, ranging from very small molecules to giant macromolecules. They analyze chemical compounds such as minerals and sugars. Biochemists deal with problems in genetics, enzymology, hormone action and bioenergetics, and they work with the phenomena of biochemical control.

Foremost among the areas of application of biochemistry are medicine, biomedicine, nutrition and agriculture. In the medical field, biochemists may investigate the causes and cures of disease, or they may develop diagnostic procedures. In the biomedical area, they contribute to our understanding of genetics, heredity, brain function and physiological adaptation. In the nutritional field, they may identify the nutrients necessary to maintain good health and the effects of specific deficiencies on various kinds of performance, including the ability to learn. In agriculture, biochemists investigate soils, fertilizers and plants; undertake studies to discover more efficient methods of crop cultivation, storage and utilization; and design and direct the use of pest-control systems.

Biochemists apply the principles and procedures of chemical and physical analysis to their research problems. Routine laboratory tasks include weighing, filtering, distilling, drying and culturing substances or materials. Some experiments require more sophisticated tasks, such as designing and constructing chemical apparatus or performing tests using radioactive tracers. Biochemists use a variety of instruments, including electron microscopes and radioactive isotope counters, and they devise new instruments and analytical techniques as needed.

Embryologists study the development of an organism from fertilization of the egg through the hatching process, or gestation period. They investigate the physiologi-

135

cal, biochemical and genetic mechanisms that control and direct the processes of development, how and why this control is accomplished and the causes of abnormalities in development.

This is a field of growing importance as concern increases about the effects of drugs, food additives and contaminating chemicals on the unborn.

Geneticists explore the origin, transmission and development of hereditary characteristics. While the traditional work of geneticists has been primarily to work in improving plant and animal breeds of economic importance, an increasing number of these scientists are becoming involved in the extremely important area of consumer protection. As scientists delve into the effects of certain substances as mutagens—heredity-changing chemicals—and the effects of radiation, the geneticist finds himself carrying out work that can have fateful consequences for mankind.

Marine Biologists may also be called fisheries biologists, fisheries research biologists, biologic oceanographers or fish conservationists. In any of these areas, a marine biologist enters the field of consumer protection with his work in studying contamination of marine life by chemicals such as mercury. As man turns increasingly to fish to feed a hungry world, this aspect of the marine biologist's work becomes more important.

Microbiologists investigate the growth, structure and general characteristics of bacteria, viruses, molds and other organisms of microscopic or submicroscopic size. Although the terms bacteriology and microbiology are sometimes used interchangeably, microbiology is the broader term and is preferable when referring to the study of all microscopic organisms. Microbiologists isolate and make cultures of these organisms in order to examine them with a variety of highly specialized equipment. Some microbiologists pursue medical problems, such as the relationship between bacteria and infectious disease or the effect of antibiotics on bacteria. Others specialize in soil bacteriology (the study of soil microorganisms and their relation to soil fertility), virology (the study of viruses), immunology (the study of the mechanisms that fight infection) or serology (the study of animal and plant fluids, including blood serums).

Pathologists are deeply involved in many fundamental phases of protecting the consumer's health. Their work consists of studying the nature, cause and development of disease, degeneration and abnormal functioning in humans, animals or plants. Many specialize in the study of the effects of diseases, parasites and insect pests on cells, tissues and organs. Other pathologists investigate genetic variations and other abnormal effects caused by drugs.

Pharmacologists conduct tests with animals such as rats, guinea pigs and monkeys to determine the effects of drugs, gases, poisons, dusts and other substances on the functioning of tissues and organs, and they relate

137

their findings with medical data. They may develop new or improved chemical compounds for use in drugs and medicines.

Physiologists study the structure and functions of cells, tissues and organs and the effects of environmental factors on life processes. They may specialize in cellular activities or in one of the organ systems, such as the digestive, nervous, circulatory or reproductive systems. The knowledge gained in such research often provides the basis for the work of many other specialists, such as biochemists, pathologists, pharmacologists or nutritionists.

Food Scientists

Food scientists or food technologists, as they are sometimes called, are in a strategic position to protect the consumer's interests, for they carry out many vital activities in every branch of the food industry.

Food scientists investigate the fundamental chemical, physical and biological nature of food, and apply this knowledge to processing, preserving and storing an adequate, nutritious and wholesome food supply. About two-fifths of all the scientists in food processing are employed in basic or applied research and development. Others work in quality-assurance laboratories, or in the production or processing areas of food plants. Some teach or do basic research in colleges and universities.

138

Food scientists in basic research study the structure and composition of foods and their changes in processing or storage. For example, they may be interested in developing new sources of proteins, studying the effects of food processing on microorganisms or searching for factors that affect the flavor, texture or appearance of foods.

In applied research and development, food scientists create new foods and develop processes for new products. They also improve existing foods by making them more nutritious and enhancing their flavor, color or texture. These scientists may formulate an idea for a new product or modify an existing item.

The food scientist must insure that each new product will retain its characteristics and nutritive value during storage. He may test additives for purity, investigate changes that take place during processing or storage or develop mass-feeding methods for food service institutions. Food scientists also maintain records of their work and prepare reports showing results of tests or experiments.

Food scientists in quality-control laboratories check raw ingredients to note freshness, maturity or suitability for processing. For example, the product may be tested for tenderness by using machines that gauge the amount of force necessary to shear or puncture the item. Periodically, the food scientists inspect processing-line operations and perform chemical and bacteriological tests

139

during and after processing to insure conformity with established industry and governmental standards. These tests vary according to the product and processing method. Canned goods, for example, may be tested for sugar, starch, protein, fat and mineral content. In a frozen-food plant, the scientist must determine that various enzymes are inactive after the product has been processed so that the food does not lose its flavor during storage. Other scientists are concerned with packaging materials to maintain their shelf life and product stability.

Whether in research or quality control, food scientists must be familiar with fundamental research techniques and standard testing equipment, such as vacuum gauges and reflectance meters.

Food scientists engaged in production and processing schedule processing operations, prepare production specifications, maintain proper temperature and humidity in storage areas and supervise sanitation, including the efficient and economical disposal of wastes. Food scientists are responsible for ways to increase processing efficiency. For example, they may advise management on the purchase of equipment, as well as recommend new sources of materials.

A bachelor's degree, with a major in food science or in one of the physical or life sciences such as chemistry or biology, is the usual minimum educational requirement for a beginning food scientist. Graduate training is essential for many positions, particularly research and college teaching, and for many management level jobs in industry.

Nearly forty colleges and universities throughout the United States offer training leading to the bachelor's degree in food science. Undergraduate courses generally include food chemistry, analysis, microbiology, engineering and processing. They also include other physical sciences such as physics and mathematics, the social sciences and humanities and business administration.

Advanced degrees are offered by most of those colleges and universities that provide undergraduate food science programs. In graduate school, students usually specialize in a particular area of food science. Requirements for the master's or doctor's degree vary by institution, but usually include laboratory work and a thesis.

A food scientist with a bachelor's degree might start work in production as a quality-assurance chemist or an assistant-production manager. After obtaining sufficient experience, the food scientist in production could advance to more responsible management positions. The scientist also might begin as a junior food chemist in the applied research and development laboratory of a food company and be promoted to section head or other research management positions.

Graduates who have a master's degree might begin

141

as senior food chemists in research and development. Graduates who have a Ph.d. probably would begin their careers doing advanced research.

Chemists

Your work as a chemist engaged in some aspect of consumer protection would be much like that of a chemist working in some other field. You would be carrying out the tasks that have brought so many wonders to our modern technology. Chemists investigate the properties and composition of matter and the laws that govern the combination of elements. They search for new knowledge about substances and try to utilize this knowledge for practical use. In conducting studies, they apply scientific principles and techniques and use a variety of specialized instruments to measure, identify and evaluate changes in matter.

A bachelor's degree with a major in chemistry is usually the minimum educational requirement for starting a career as a chemist. Graduate training is essential for many positions. Training leading to a bachelor's degree is offered by more than 1,000 colleges and universities. In addition to the required chemistry courses in analytical, inorganic, organic and physical chemistry, the undergraduate chemistry major also takes courses in mathematics (particularly analytical geometry and calculus) and physics.

Advanced degrees in chemistry are awarded at about 300 colleges and universities. Many of these offer financial assistance to students interested in graduate study. In graduate school the student generally specializes by taking several courses in a particular field of chemistry. Requirements for the master's or doctor's degree vary by institution, but usually include a thesis based on independent research.

New graduates having the bachelor's degree usually qualify for beginning positions in analysis and testing, quality control and technical service and sales, or they assist senior chemists in research and development work. Most chemists having only the bachelor's degree start their careers in industry or government. In industry, employers often have special training programs for new chemistry graduates. These programs supplement college training with specific industry techniques and help determine the type of work for which the new employee is best suited. Some chemists who have a bachelor's degree teach or do research in colleges and universities while working toward advanced degrees. They also may qualify as secondary school teachers.

Chemists having a master's degree often qualify for applied research positions in government or private industry. They also may qualify for some teaching positions in colleges and universities and in two-year colleges.

The salaries of chemists vary somewhat, depending on the employer. However, the general range of salaries is

143

similar to that of other professions: $9,000 to $11,000 as starting salary for the holder of a bachelor's degree, $14,000 for someone with a master's, considerably more for a Ph.d.

Physicists

In a world increasingly subject to possible harmful radiation, the physicist has his work cut out for him. However, the scope of a modern physicist's activities goes far beyond dealing with the menace of radiation. With their specialized knowledge of the nature of matter and energy, physicists are often members of a team working in some phase of product safety. Physicists contribute to the work of biologists, chemists, food scientists and virtually all kinds of engineers.

A bachelor's degree is the minimum requirement for a career in physics, but most scientists entering this field feel that major achievement is not possible without an advanced degree.

Physicists having bachelor's degrees qualify for a variety of jobs in applied research and development work with either private industry or the federal government. Some become research assistants in colleges and universities while working toward advanced degrees. Many persons having a bachelor's degree in the sciences do not work as physicists, but enter nontechnical work, other sciences or engineering.

144

Science Careers in Consumer Protection

Over 800 colleges and universities offer training leading to the bachelor's degree in physics. In addition, many engineering schools offer a physics major as part of the general curriculum. The undergraduate program in physics provides a broad background in the science, which serves as a base for later specialization, either in graduate school or on the job. A few of the physics courses typically offered in an undergraduate program are mechanics, electricity, magnetics, optics, thermodynamics and atomic and molecular physics. In addition, courses in chemistry and mathematics are required.

Approximately 250 colleges and universities offer advanced degrees in physics. In graduate school, the student—with faculty guidance—usually works in a specific field. The graduate student, especially the candidate for the Ph.d. degree, spends a large portion of his or her time in research. After graduation he or she can expect to work for any of countless different kinds of private industries or for a number of different governmental agencies, including those concerned with consumer protection.

The salaries of physicists are rising, along with those of scientists in all fields. Starting salaries are over $10,000 for those with bachelor's degrees; $12,000 and up for those with advanced degrees. Possible top earnings for physicists probably run somewhat ahead of those in other fields, with salaries upwards of $30,000 not uncommon.

7. Engineering Careers in Consumer Protection

All the resources of modern science and technology are waiting to be applied to the manufacture of humanly designed and constructed products. It is up to us to take advantage of them.

Ralph Nader

Recognition that engineering can play a major part in helping the consumer can provide a new challenge to anyone considering an engineering career. Engineers carry out two broad tasks in consumer protection: they *design* better, safer, more durable products—ranging from aerosol cans to automobiles—and they *test* the thousands of products that pour from factories, to see that they meet the standards that qualify them to meet consumer needs.

Carrying out one or both of these roles promises new

146

satisfactions for the young man or woman who goes into engineering. These satisfactions are available not only to those who go to work for some consumer-protection agency or organization, but also to many who go to work for private industry, still the largest area of employment for engineers.

"When I first thought of going into engineering," says a young engineer who now works for an appliance maker,

> the thought that really turned me off was the feeling that the companies I might work for were simply going to put me to work designing new gadgets, aimed at making more money—not giving the consumer a break at all. You know the kind of thing. Design a product or a part of a product to break down at a certain time. Don't pay any attention to how safe it is. I didn't think I could live with that. Fortunately, I found I didn't have to. The company that gave me my first job has seen the light. I think they're genuinely trying to do something for the consumer. My job is to work with some senior engineers in completely redesigning the company's major product. We've been given a green light to go ahead and do away with the factors in it that consumers have been complaining about for years—with no results.

The basic nature of engineering has not been changed

by new goals, though. It is still a practical, problem-solving profession that consists of figuring out the best way to do something. To be an engineer, you need initiative, an analytical mind, a capacity for detail and the ability to make decisions. Actually, an engineer is often something of an inventor, an innovator. Many of the problems confronting engineers do not boil down to mere sets of figures. They call for special solutions which the engineer must "invent."

To become an engineer, you will need a minimum of a bachelor's degree. About 270 colleges, universities and engineering schools offer a bachelor's degree in engineering. These educational institutions offer nearly 1,000 curriculum choices. Although the larger branches of engineering are offered in most schools, some specialties are taught in only relatively few institutions. If you desire to specialize, you should investigate various curriculums before selecting a college. For undergraduate admission, engineering schools usually require high school courses in mathematics and the physical sciences.

In the typical four-year curriculum, the first two years are spent mainly on basic science—mathematics, physics and chemistry—and the humanities, social sciences and English. The last two years are devoted chiefly to engineering, with emphasis on a specialty. Some programs, however, offer general training; the student chooses a specialty in graduate school or acquires one on the job.

Some engineering curriculums require more than four

years to complete. However, the number of institutions having five-year programs leading to the bachelor's degree is decreasing. Several engineering schools now have formal arrangements with liberal arts colleges whereby a student spends three years in liberal arts and two years in engineering and receives a bachelor's degree from each. This program offers the student diversification in his studies.

Some institutions have five- or six-year cooperative plans under which a student alternates school and employment. Most of these plans coordinate classroom study and practical experience. In this way, the student may finance part of his education in addition to gaining experience.

Engineering graduates usually begin work as trainees or as assistants to experienced engineers. Many large companies have programs designed to acquaint new engineers with special industrial practices and to determine the specialty for which they are best suited. As they gain experience, engineers may advance to positions of greater responsibility. Those with proven ability often become administrators. Increasingly large numbers of engineers are promoted to top executive posts. Many engineers obtain graduate degrees in business administration to improve their advancement opportunities.

Prospective engineers should be able to communicate their ideas to specialists in areas such as marketing and production planning. The ability to cut across various

149

disciplines and systematically evaluate and solve problems is also important. Because of rapidly changing technologies, an engineer must be willing to continue his education throughout his career.

As is the case in all professions, salaries of engineers are rising rapidly. There are some minor variations in the salaries of various engineering professions, but in general they are about equal. In 1974, starting salaries of engineers in private employment were about $11,000. Average salaries for experienced engineers were generally upwards of $15,000, with many engineers earning $30,000 and more.

In the 1960s, there was some indication that there were "too many engineers." In the 1970s that situation has changed. Conservative estimates all indicate that, for decades to come, we will need more engineers than ever in almost all categories. The opportunity to find a career in some phase of engineering that concerns consumer protection is even more wide open than some of the older aspects of this profession. Let's glance at some of the kinds of engineers who will be in positions where they can do something for the consumer.

Agricultural Engineers

As an agricultural engineer working in traditional fields, you would use basic engineering principles and concepts to develop machinery, equipment and methods to improve the efficiency and economy of the production, processing and distribution of food and other agricultural products. You would be concerned with the design of farm machinery, equipment and structures; the utilization of electrical energy on farms and in food and feed processing plants; the conservation of soil and water resources; and the design and operation of processing equipment to prepare agricultural products for market.

As an agricultural engineer you might help protect the consumer by developing alternatives to the use of pesticides and herbicides which can contaminate food products. One young engineer, for example, developed a machine that could burn off weeds in a controlled manner and without injuring nearby crop rows, thus eliminating the need for herbicides. Another engineer aided biological scientists in devising a trap that destroyed insects by attracting them with black light. It was part of a system designed to eliminate the use of pesticides to kill insects. In another area, it was an agricultural engineer who developed a rodent-proof storage building that did away with the problem of contamination of stored foods by rodents.

Chemical Engineers

As a chemical engineer your traditional activity would be to design plants and equipment to manufacture chemicals and chemical products, and to determine

151

the most efficient manufacturing processes. Your work would extend far beyond the laboratory, for you would also design and operate pilot plants—miniature factories that would get the "bugs" out of procedures before they are put into actual operation. To these basic tasks of the chemical engineer has been added the assignment of making chemical operations not only efficient but environmentally sound.

Chemical engineers make many direct and indirect contributions to consumer protection. As such an engineer, you might participate in the design of a food processing plant or a process that will keep foods from being contaminated. You might help design pharmaceutical processing equipment that insures the purity of drugs. Or you could assist in the design of testing apparatus for food and drug products. As an inspector, working either for private industry or a governmental agency, you would be employing your knowledge and skill to detect flaws in manufacturing methods that could result in contamination of food and drug products.

Civil Engineers

Civil engineers are the builders of the engineering team, the ones who figure out the "make-it-work" details that permit the construction of roads, harbors, airfields, tunnels, bridges, large buildings and water supply and sewage systems.

Engineering Careers in Consumer Protection

As a civil engineer your role in consumer protection would probably be an indirect one, concerned with environmental factors. An example would be the part engineers are playing in developing safe, pollution-free mass transport systems. In the future many civil engineers will play a more direct part in consumer protection as building inspectors.

Electrical Engineers

The basic work of the electrical engineer consists of designing, developing and supervising the manufacture of electrical and electronic equipment, including electric motors and generators, communications equipment, electronic apparatus such as televisions, computers and missile guidance systems and electrical appliances of all kinds. Another broad field is the design, construction and operation of facilities for generating and distributing electric power.

The consumer protection work of the electrical engineer would be mainly in the area of product safety and durability. An increasingly large number of firms that make electrical appliances are assigning electrical engineers to the task of devising better and safer products. Testing these products in company laboratories and in government and private labs is a major activity of electrical engineers.

CAREERS IN CONSUMER PROTECTION

Mechanical Engineers

Mechanical engineers carry out hundreds of tasks in fields that include every aspect of modern technology. They are concerned with the production, transmission and use of power. They design and develop machines which produce power, such as internal combustion engines, steam and gas turbines, jet and rocket engines and nuclear reactors. They also design and develop a great variety of machines that use power—refrigeration and air-conditioning equipment, elevators, machine tools, printing presses, steel-rolling mills, and so on—through a list that includes hundreds of kinds of machines.

In an age of consumer outrage over machines—from automobiles to toys—that break down, wear out too soon and often endanger their users, mechanical engineers play an increasingly important part in consumer protection. "Machines designed for consumers—not for industrial convenience" is the new slogan that is spreading through industry. The mechanical engineers who work in the many specialties blanketed under this term will not only get a chance to design consumer-oriented machines, but will also get to test them as well. Mechanical engineers are the largest category of engineer employees of the test laboratories which prove whether the machines really do what they are supposed to do, reliably and safely.

8. Technicians—Non-College Careers in Consumer Protection

Tracking down a dangerous organism in a food product.

Carrying out an analysis of a new drug.

Working on a team that develops a new kind of flameproofing for children's garments.

Conducting tests of a household appliance.

These are samples of the challenging activities you might be involved in if you go into one of the careers in consumer protection that do not require college degrees. Most of the work in consumer protection, which includes so many professions, is carried out by college graduates. However, by becoming a technician, a non-college graduate can find many opportunities to have a meaningful career, doing important work that will help protect the consumer.

The term "technician" is a rather elastic one used to describe various jobs in science and engineering. In some industries the term is applied to employees doing routine work that requires little knowledge or training. However, the technicians whose work we describe here are those who have enough training to be considered assistants to scientists and engineers. To get such a position in a government agency, pharmaceutical plant, independent testing agency or food processing firm, where most technician opportunities exist, you will need some kind of specific training beyond your high school education.

Where can you get such training? Fortunately, it is available from a great variety of educational institutions. They include technical institutes, technical-vocational schools, junior and community colleges and extension divisions of colleges and universities.

You may also get to be a technician by taking correspondence courses or through training and experience obtained while serving in the Armed Forces. In addition, many engineering and science students who have had some college, but who have not completed all the requirements for a bachelor's degree, are able to qualify for responsible technician jobs after they obtain some additional technical training and experience. Of all these alternatives, the best one for most people is formal training in a post-secondary school after graduation from high school.

For admittance to most schools offering post-secondary technician training, a high school diploma is usually required. Some schools, however, admit students without a high school diploma if they are able to pass special examinations and can otherwise demonstrate their ability to perform work above the high school level. All engineering and science occupations require basic training in mathematics and science, so you should obtain a sound background in these subjects when in high school. Many post-secondary schools have arrangements for helping students make up deficiencies in these subjects.

Programs offered by schools specializing in post-secondary technical training require one, two, three or four years of full-time study. The majority are two-year programs leading to an associate of arts or science degree. Evening as well as day sessions are generally available. The courses offered in science, mathematics and engineering are usually at the college level. They include instruction in laboratory techniques and the use of instruments, and emphasize the practical problems met on the job. Students also are instructed in the use of machinery and tools to give them a familiarity with this equipment rather than to develop skills.

Some four-year programs for the bachelor's degree in technology place more emphasis on courses in the humanities and business administration than do the two-year programs, while other four-year programs emphasize additional technical training.

Because of the variety of educational institutions and the differences in the kind and level of education and training, persons seeking a technical education should use more than ordinary care in selecting a school. Information should be secured about the fields of technology in which training is offered, accreditation, the length of time the school has been in operation, instructional facilities, faculty qualifications, transferability of credits toward the bachelor's degree and the type of work obtained by the school's graduates.

Briefly discussed here are some of the types of post-secondary educational institutions and other facilities at which young people can obtain training as technicians.

Technical Institutes. Technical institutes offer training designed to qualify the graduate for a specific job or cluster of jobs immediately upon graduation with only a minimum of on-the-job training. In general, the student receives intensive technical training but less theoretical and general education than is provided in curriculums leading to a bachelor's degree in engineering and liberal arts colleges. A few technical institutes and community colleges offer cooperative programs in which students spend part of their time in school and part in paid employment for which they are preparing themselves.

Some technical institutes are operated as regular or extension divisions of colleges and universities. Others are separated by states or municipalities, privately endowed institutions and proprietary schools.

Junior Colleges and Community Colleges. Many junior and community colleges offer the necessary training to prepare students for technician occupations. Some of these schools offer curriculums that are similar to those given in the freshman and sophomore years of four-year colleges. Graduates can transfer after the junior college into a four-year college or qualify for some technician jobs. Most large community colleges offer two-year technical programs, and many employers express a preference for graduates having this more specialized training. Junior college courses in technical fields are often planned around the employment needs of the industries in their locality.

Area Technical-Vocational Schools. Area technical-vocational schools are post-secondary public institutions that are established in central locations to serve students from several surrounding areas. In general, the admission requirements of technical-vocational schools are as rigid as those of other schools offering post-secondary technician training. School curriculums are often designed to train the types of technicians most needed in the area.

As a "graduate" of any of these institutions for training technicians, your earning potential would not be as great as that of college graduates in the related branches of science and engineering. However, you could look forward to substantial earnings. Starting salaries range from $6,000 to $8,500, depending on the field entered and the kind and amount of training. Salaries for experienced technicians tend to increase rapidly to figures above $10,000. Salaries of $12,000 to $15,000 are unusual but attainable.

Technician careers in work related to consumer protection fall into certain broad categories. Let's take a look at those that offer the greatest possibilities:

Food Processing Technicians

Food processing technicians assist food scientists in research and development and in the quality assurance laboratories of processing plants. They also serve as assistant supervisory personnel in production-related operations such as processing, packaging and sanitary maintenance and waste disposal.

Titles of operating and laboratory technicians in the food processing industry vary from plant to plant and industry to industry, as do their responsibilities, which often overlap from one area to the next. A food processing technician may be known as a laboratory or quality assurance technician, a physical-science aide, a plant facilities technician, a biological aide, a laboratory analyst or a research and development technician.

In research and development, food processing technicians assist food scientists in improving existing food products, creating new food items and developing and improving processes related to production. Duties may include weighing out ingredients, performing microbiological tests and conducting chemical analysis. Technicians also set up panels for organoleptic testing (taste, smell, sight). Other duties include gathering and storing samples for testing, operating and maintaining laboratory equipment and experimenting with new methods for testing products. Technicians often are required to

160

prepare formal reports on experiments, tests and other projects. They frequently use instruments such as balances, spectrophotometers (to measure color intensity), autoclaves (for sterilizing), microscopes and cryoscopes (to determine the freezing point of liquids).

In quality assurance laboratories, these technicians conduct bacteriological, chemical and physical tests on raw ingredients and finished products to insure conformity with established industry and government standards. They use equipment such as incubators, refractometers (to measure heat), centrifuges (to separate particles of substances), torsion balances, color comparison charts and pH meters (to determine the degree of acidity). Other duties may include making brand comparison checks, filling sample orders and checking samples received against product reports or shipping manifests.

In production operations, food processing technicians assist in the supervision of the overall processing of food products. For example, they work closely with fieldmen to insure a steady flow of products from farm to plant; they inspect incoming raw materials to make certain they are suitable for processing and that they are stored under proper temperatures. Technicians recommend measures to improve production methods, equipment performance and quality of product, and they suggest changes in working conditions and use of equipment to increase processing efficiency. Some technicians supervise packaging operations; others are concerned primarily with sanitation in all areas of a food processing

161

plant. They help identify bacterial problems on the line or in the plant, recommend cleaning and sanitizing solutions and direct cleaning crews.

Medical Laboratory Technicians

Most medical laboratory technicians work in hospitals, but there is a place for an increasing number of them in laboratories carrying out work connected with consumer protection. As an employee of a pharmaceutical house, medical research organization, public health department or other government agency, you would be doing work similar to that of technicians in hospitals. You would be assisting pathologists, scientists and their highly trained assistants, medical technologists, in their task of measuring the possible effects of various drugs on people.

Medical laboratory workers use precision instruments such as microscopes and automatic analyzers to study the blood, tissues and fluids in the human body. Medical laboratory technicians may concentrate in one of several areas. Those working in bacteriology, serology and parasitology prepare and stain slides for study, apply sensitivity discs to culture plates and record the results. They also prepare specimens for microscopic studies. Technicians in the field of hematology—the study of the blood —perform blood counts and tests to determine bleeding time, sedimentation rate and other factors. In clinical chemistry, technicians assist in such laboratory techniques as centrifuging urine samples and preparing the samples for microscopic study.

Mechanical Technician

Mechanical technology is a broad term used to cover a large number of fields. Just as many more engineers will be required to work on aspects of machine design that improve all kinds of consumer-used devices, so will more and more mechanical technicians be required. As assistants to engineers, particularly mechanical and electrical engineers, mechanical technicians will find many opportunities to play a part in improving the safety, utility and durability of automobiles, appliances and all kinds of home equipment.

Your work as a mechanical technician would include many of the tasks carried out by engineers. You would help design machinery by making sketches and rough layouts of proposed equipment and parts. You would help test newly designed equipment for such design problems as tolerance, stress, strain, friction, vibration, noise and wear. In the testing procedure you would record data, make computations, plot graphs, analyze results and write reports.

Chemical Technician

Technicians specializing in this area work mainly with chemists and chemical engineers in the development, production, sale and utilization of chemical and related products and equipment. For example, as a technician

163

working for a company making air or water pollution analyzing equipment, you might be involved in the development or design of such equipment; you might assist in testing such equipment; you might be sent out into the field to instruct scientists, engineers and other technicians how to use it properly; you might be assigned to work with a scientific team carrying out a research program involving the equipment.

Or you might be in a laboratory, working on the analysis of air or water samples. You could also be engaged in studies of various pollutants, or suspected pollutants, measuring the amount of them present in discharges from factories.

If you became a chemical technician, you would really be an assistant chemist, carrying out just about all the operations assigned to members of this profession. Chemical technicians have an important place in many aspects of consumer protection, particularly in the pharmaceutical field. Here you would most likely be engaged in the routine tasks connected with the manufacture of drugs which meet the high standards of purity required. However, your work might well take you into the increasingly important area of checking out new drugs for safety during their period of evaluation.

You might also be employed by a public health laboratory, where you would be directly on the firing line of consumer protection as you analyzed food contaminants and explored the dangerous potentials of chemical products.

Epilogue

The future in consumer protection would not hold the exciting career promise it does if its scope were limited to the organizations, governmental and private, dedicated to consumer interests. Important as the role of these organizations is, the real success of consumer protection comes down to how much energy American business and industry are willing to throw into improving their products and services.

Fortunately, American business and industry are accepting the concept that they must take a new approach to consumers.

"As businessmen our focus must be on the quality of the service or product we offer, simply because that is the first expectation people have of us," says Edward R. Rust, president of the Chamber of Commerce of the United States.

The manufacturer who landscapes the factory site but hedges the obligations in his product warranty has a misplaced sense of priorities. It's at this basic level that we must begin to rebuild faith in the institution of business. We need to regenerate a dedication to quality, to value and to service. We need a commitment to excellence first of all in those things in which we are best equipped to excel. The business manager may need instruction in some of the new social roles that are being urged upon him —but he should need no instruction at all in bringing to the marketplace a product or service that meets whatever claims he is willing to make for it.

This attitude on the part of industry may mean that fewer workers will be required in the regulatory agencies that now protect consumers, but it does mean that there will be many more meaningful career opportunities open to tomorrow's consumer protectors in actually designing cars and toys and appliances, in developing and testing drugs, in raising and processing food and in building houses—the places where consumer protection should really begin.

Suggested Further Readings

Asker, David A. and Day, G. S. *Consumerism: Search for the Consumer Interest.* N.Y.: Free Press, 1971.

Battista, Orlando A. *Challenge of Chemistry.* N.Y.: Holt, Rinehart and Winston.

Bayliss, Sylvia, et al., eds. *Career Opportunities: Community Services and Related Specialists.* N.Y.: Doubleday, 1970.

Bell, Raymond M. *Your Future in Physics.* N.Y.: Richards Rosen Press, 1967.

Binkley, Harold R. and Hammond, Carsie. *Experience Programs for Learning Vocations in Agriculture.* Danville, Illinois: Interstate, 1970.

Bishop, James and Hubbard, Henry. *Let the Seller Beware.* Palo Alto, Calif.: National Press.

Brooking, Walter J., ed. *Career Opportunities: Engineering Technicians.* N.Y.: Doubleday.

Brown, Theodore. *Energy and the Environment.* Columbus, Ohio: Charles E. Merrill, 1971.

Buckhorn, Robert F. *Nader: The People's Lawyer.* Englewood Cliffs, N.J.: Prentice-Hall, 1972.

Byram, Harold M. *Guidance in Agricultural Education.* Danville, Illinois: Interstate, 1966.

CAREERS IN CONSUMER PROTECTION

Dowdell, Dorothy and Dowdell, Joseph. *Careers in Horticultural Sciences*. N.Y.: Julian Messner, 1969.

Fuller, John G. *200,000,000 Guinea Pigs*. N.Y.: G. P. Putnam's Sons, 1972.

Hey, Nigel. *How Will we Feed the Hungry Billions?* N.Y.: Julian Messner, 1971.

Hoover, Norman K. *Handbook of Agricultural Occupations*. Danville, Illinois: Interstate, 1969.

Hunter, Beatrice Trum. *Consumer Beware!* N.Y.: Simon & Schuster, 1971.

Hutchison, Chester S. *Your Future in Agriculture*. N.Y.: Richards Rosen Press, 1971.

Levy, Leon; Feldman, Robert; and Sasserath, Simpson. *The Consumer in the Marketplace*. N.Y.: Pitman Publishing.

Liston, Robert A. *Your Career in Civil Service*. N.Y.: Julian Messner, 1966.

Margolius, Sidney. *The Innocent Consumer Vs. The Exploiters*. N.Y.: Trident Press, 1967.

Mather, Loys I., ed. *Economics of Consumer Protection*. Danville, Illinois: Interstate.

McClellan, Grant S., ed. *The Consuming Public*. N.Y.: H. W. Wilson, 1968.

Michelsohn, David Reuben. *Housing in Tomorrow's World*. N.Y.: Julian Messner, 1973.

Millard, Reed. *Careers In Environmental Protection*. N.Y.: Julian Messner, 1974.

Nadel, Mark. *Politics of Consumer Protection*. Indianapolis: Bobbs-Merrill, 1971.

Nader, Ralph. *Unsafe At any Speed*. Rev. ed. N.Y.: Grossman, 1972.

Neal, Harry E. *Engineers Unlimited: Your Career in Engineering*. N.Y.: Julian Messner, 1968.

Nourse, Alan E. *So You Want to Be a Physicist*. N.Y.: Harper & Row, 1963.

Nourse, Alan E. and Webbert, James C. *So You Want to Be a Chemist.* N.Y.: Harper & Row, 1964.

Paris, Jeanne. *Your Future as a Home Economist.* N.Y.: Arco, 1964.

Peterson, Mary Bennett. *Regulated Consumer.* Freeport, N.Y.: Nash, 1971.

Pollack, Philip. *Careers and Opportunities in Chemistry.* N.Y.: E. P. Dutton.

————. *Careers and Opportunities in Physics.* N.Y.: E. P. Dutton, 1961.

Pollack, Philip and Alden, John. *Careers and Opportunities in Engineering.* N.Y.: E. P. Dutton, 1967.

Schoenfeld, David and Natella, Arthur. *The Consumer and His Dollars.* Dobbs Ferry, N.Y.: Oceana Publications, 1970.

Schrag, Philip G. *Counsel for the Deceived: Case Studies in Consumer Fraud.* N.Y.: Pantheon, 1972.

Sidney, Howard, ed. *Career Opportunities: Agricultural, Forestry and Oceanographic Technicians.* N.Y.: Doubleday.

Smith, Ralph. *Engineering as a Career.* N.Y.: McGraw-Hill, 1969.

Swanson, Harold. *Looking Forward to a Career: Agriculture.* Minneapolis: Dillon Press, 1970.

Turner, James S. *The Chemical Feast,* N.Y.: Grossman, 1970.

U.S. Department of Agriculture. *Consumers All.* U.S. Gov't Printing Office.

U.S. Department of Agriculture. *Protecting our Food.* USDA.

U.S. Office of Consumer Affairs. *Consumer Education Bibliography.* U.S. Gov't Printing Office.

Wellford, Harrison. *Sowing The Wind.* N.Y.: Grossman, 1972.

Winter, Charles A. *Opportunities in the Biological Sciences.* N.Y.: Universal Publishing & Distributing Co.

Woodburn, John H. *Opportunities in the Chemical Sciences.* N.Y.: Universal Publishing & Distributing, Co., 1971.

Sources of Further Information

SOCIETIES THAT PROVIDE INFORMATION ABOUT CAREERS AND EDUCATIONAL FACILITIES

CHEMISTRY

American Chemical Society
1155 16th St. N.W.
Washington, D.C. 20036

Manufacturing Chemists' Association, Inc.
1825 Connecticut Ave. N.W.
Washington, D.C. 20009

ENGINEERING

American Institute of Aeronautics and Astronautics, Inc.
1290 Avenue of the Americas
New York, N.Y. 10019

American Institute of Chemical Engineers
345 E. 47th St.
New York, N.Y. 10017

170

Sources of Further Information

American Institute of Industrial Engineers, Inc.
345 E. 47th St.
New York, N.Y. 10017

American Society of Agricultural Engineers
2950 Niles Road
St. Joseph, Mo. 49085

American Society of Civil Engineers
345 E. 47th St.
New York, N.Y. 10017

American Society of Mechanical Engineers
345 E. 47th St.
New York, N.Y. 10017

American Society of Metals
Metals Park, Oh. 44073

Engineering Manpower Commission
Engineers Joint Council
345 E. 47th St.
New York, N.Y. 10017

Engineers' Council for Professional Development
345 E. 47th St.
New York, N.Y. 10017

Institute of Electrical and Electronic Engineers
345 E. 47th St.
New York, N.Y. 10017

National Society of Professional Engineers
2029 K St. N.W.
Washington, D.C. 20006

ENGINEERING AND SCIENCE TECHNOLOGY

American Society for Engineering Education
1 Dupont Circle, Suite 400
Washington, D.C. 20036

CAREERS IN CONSUMER PROTECTION

Engineers' Council for Professional Development
345 E. 47th St.
New York, N.Y. 10017

National Council of Technical Schools
1835 K St. N.W., Room 907
Washington, D.C. 20006

HOME ECONOMICS

American Home Economics Association
2010 Massachusetts Ave. N.W.
Washington, D.C. 20036

Bureau of Adult, Vocational and Technical Education
U.S. Department of Health, Education and Welfare
Washington, D.C. 20202

INDUSTRIAL HYGIENE

National Institute of Environmental Health Sciences
Research Triangle Park, N.C. 27709

LIFE SCIENCES

American Institute of Biological Sciences
3900 Wisconsin Ave. N.W.
Washington, D.C. 20016

American Physiological Society
9650 Rockville Pike
Bethesda, Md. 20014

American Society of Biological Chemists
9650 Rockville Pike
Bethesda, Md. 20014

American Society of Horticultural Science
615 Elm St.
St. Joseph, Mo. 49085

American Veterinary Medical Association
600 S. Michigan Ave.
Chicago, Ill. 60605

Ecological Society of America
Connecticut College
New London, Conn. 06320

NUTRITION AND FOOD SCIENCE

The American Dietetic Association
620 N. Michigan Ave.
Chicago, Ill. 60611

The Institute of Food Technologists
231 N. LaSalle St.
Chicago, Ill. 60601

PHARMACEUTICS

American Association of Colleges of Pharmacy
8121 Georgia Ave.
Silver Spring, Md. 20910

American Council on Pharmaceutical Education
77 W. Washington St.
Chicago, Ill. 60602

PHYSICS

American Institute of Physics
335 E. 45th St.
New York, N.Y. 10017

FEDERAL AGENCIES CONCERNED WITH CONSUMER PROTECTION

Agricultural Research Service
Beltsville, Md. 20782

CAREERS IN CONSUMER PROTECTION

Atomic Energy Commission
Washington, D.C. 20545

Bureau of Family Services
Washington, D.C. 20201

Bureau of Radiological Health
Washington, D.C. 20201

Consumer and Marketing Service, USDA
516 S. Clark St.
Chicago, Ill. 60605

Consumer Product Information Coordinating Center
Arlington, Va. 22210

Consumer Products Safety Commission
Washington, D.C. 20207

Department of Commerce
Washington, D.C. 20230

Department of Health, Education and Welfare
Washington, D.C. 20201

Department of Housing and Urban Development
Washington, D.C. 20410

Department of Transportation
Washington, D.C. 20590

Environmental Protection Agency
Washington, D.C. 20590

Federal Extension Service
Washington, D.C. 20250

Federal Housing Administration
Washington, D.C. 20410

Federal Trade Commission
Washington, D.C. 20204

Food and Drug Administration
Washington, D.C. 20201

Institute of Home Economics
Beltsville, Md. 20782

National Bureau of Standards
Washington, D.C. 20204

National Highway Traffic Safety Administration
Department of Transportation
Washington, D.C. 20590

Occupational Safety and Health Administration
Washington, D.C. 20210

Office of Consumer Affairs
Washington, D.C. 20204

Office of Product Safety
Washington, D.C. 20204

Public Health Service
Washington, D.C. 20201

STATE CONSUMER PROTECTION AGENCIES

Alabama
  Attorney General
  State of Alabama
  Montgomery, Ala. 36104

Alaska
  Attorney General of Alaska
  Pouch "K", State Capitol
  Juneau, Alas. 99801

Arizona
  Assistant Attorney General in Charge
    Consumer Fraud Division
  159 State Capitol Bldg.
  Phoenix, Ariz. 85007

Arkansas
Assistant Attorney General in Charge
  Consumer Protection
Justice Bldg.
Little Rock, Ark. 72201

California
Attorney General of California
500 Wells Fargo Bank Bldg.
Sacramento, Calif. 95814

Director
Department of Consumer Affairs
1020 N Street
Sacramento, Calif. 95814

Colorado
Assistant Attorney General
Office of Consumer Affairs
503 Farmers Union Bldg.
1575 Sherman Street
Denver, Colo. 80203

Connecticut
Commissioner
Department of Consumer Protection
State Office Bldg.
Hartford, Conn. 06115

Delaware
Deputy Attorney General
Consumer Protection Division
1206 King Street
Wilmington, Del. 19801

Director
Division of Consumer Affairs
704 Delaware Avenue
Wilmington, Del. 19801

176

Florida
   Attorney General of Florida
   State Capitol
   Tallahassee, Fla. 32304

   Director
   Division of Consumer Affairs
   Florida Department of Agriculture
      and Consumer Services
   State Capitol
   Tallahassee, Fla. 32304

Georgia
   Program Director
   Georgia Consumer Services Program
   15 Peachtree Street, Room 909
   Atlanta, Ga. 30303

Hawaii
   Director of Consumer Protection
   Office of the Governor
   P.O. Box 3767
   Honolulu, Hawaii 96811

Idaho
   Assistant Attorney General in charge
      of Consumer Protection Division
   State Capitol
   Boise, Idaho 83707

Illinois
   Assistant Attorney General and Chief
   Consumer Fraud Section
   134 North La Salle Street, Room 204
   Chicago, Ill. 60602

177

Indiana
  Director
  Office of Consumer Protection
  Attorney General of Indiana
  219 State House
  Indianapolis, Ind. 46204

  Director
  Consumer Advisory Council
  c/o Indiana Department of Commerce
  336 State House
  Indianapolis, Ind. 46204

Iowa
  Assistant Attorney General
  Consumer Protection Division
  20 East 13th Court
  Des Moines, Iowa 50319

Kansas
  Assistant Attorney General in charge
     of Consumer Protection
  State House
  Topeka, Kan. 66612

Kentucky
  Assistant Attorney General
  Consumer Protection Division
  State Capitol
  Frankfort, Ky. 40601

  Executive Director
  Citizen's Commission for Consumer Protection
  State Capitol
  Frankfort, Ky. 40601

Louisiana
  Attorney General
  State of Louisiana
  State Capitol
  Baton Rouge, La. 70804

Maine
  Assistant Attorney General
  Consumer Protection Division
  State House
  Augusta, Me. 04330

Maryland
  Assistant Attorney General and Chief
  Consumer Protection Division
  1200 One Charles Center
  Baltimore, Md. 21201

Massachusetts
  Consumer Protection Division
  Office of Attorney General
  State House
  Boston, Mass. 02133

  Executive Secretary
  Massachusetts Consumers' Council
  State Office Bldg.
  100 Cambridge Street
  Boston, Mass. 02202

Michigan
  Assistant Attorney General in charge of
    Consumer Protection
  Law Bldg.
  Lansing, Mich. 48902

Special Assistant to the Governor for
  Consumer Affairs
1033 South Washington Street
Lansing, Mich. 48910

Executive Director
Michigan Consumer Council
525 Hollister Bldg.
Lansing, Mich, 48933

Minnesota
Special Assistant
Attorney General for Consumer Protection
102 State Capitol
St. Paul, Minn. 55101

Director
Office of Consumer Services
Department of Commerce, Room 230
State Office Bldg.
St. Paul, Minn. 55101

Mississippi
Assistant Attorney General in charge of
  Consumer Protection
State Capitol
Jackson, Miss. 39201

Consumer Protection Division
Department of Agriculture and Commerce
Jackson, Miss. 39205

Missouri
Assistant Attorney General
Consumer Protection Division
Supreme Court Bldg.
Jefferson City, Mo. 65101

Montana
  Attorney General
  State of Montana
  Capitol Bldg.
  Helena, Mont. 59601

Nebraska
  Attorney General
  State of Nebraska
  State Capitol
  Lincoln, Neb. 68509

Nevada
  Attorney General
  State of Nevada
  Supreme Court Bldg.
  Carson City, Nev. 89701

New Hampshire
  Attorney General
  State of New Hampshire
  State House Annex
  Concord, N.H. 03301

New Jersey
  Attorney General
  State of New Jersey
  State House Annex
  Trenton, N.J. 08625

  Director
  Office of Consumer Protection
  1100 Raymond Bldg.
  Newark, N.J. 07102

New Mexico
  Consumer Protection Division
  Lamy Bldg.
  Santa Fe, N.M. 87501

CAREERS IN CONSUMER PROTECTION

New York
  Assistant Attorney General in Charge
    Consumer Frauds and Protection Bureau
  80 Centre Street
  New York, N.Y. 10013

  Bureau of Consumer Fraud
  State of New York
  Department of Law
  300 Terminal Bldg.
  65 Broad Street
  Rochester, N.Y. 14614

  Assistant Attorney General
  Department of Law
  65 Court Street
  Buffalo, N.Y. 14202

  Consumer Protection Board
  380 Madison Avenue
  New York, N.Y. 10017

North Carolina
  Deputy Attorney General
  Consumer Protection Division
  P.O. Box 629
  Raleigh, N.C. 27602

North Dakota
  Assistant Attorney General
  Consumer Protection Division
  The Capitol
  Bismarck, N.D. 58501

Ohio
  Assistant Attorney General and Chief
    Consumer Frauds and Crimes Section
  State House Annex
  Columbus, Oh. 43215

182

Oklahoma
   Administrator
   Department of Consumer Affairs
   Lincoln Office Plaza, Suite 74
   4545 Lincoln Blvd.
   Oklahoma City, Okla. 73105

Oregon
   Special Assistant Attorney General
   Antitrust and Consumer Protection
   322 State Office Bldg.
   Salem, Ore. 97310

   Assistant to the Governor
   Economic Development and Consumer Services
   State Capitol Bldg.
   Salem, Ore. 97301

Pennsylvania
   Director
   Bureau of Consumer Protection
   Pennsylvania Department of Justice
   2-4 North Market Square
   Harrisburg, Pa. 17101

   Bureau of Consumer Protection
   711 State Office Bldg.
   Philadelphia, Pa. 19107

   Bureau of Consumer Protection
   1405 State Office Bldg.
   Pittsburgh, Pa. 15222

Rhode Island
   Consumer Affairs Section
   Attorney General's Office
   Providence County Court House
   Providence, R.I. 02903

183

Executive Director
Rhode Island Consumers' Council
365 Broadway
Providence, R.I. 02902

South Carolina
　Attorney General
　State of South Carolina
　Hampton Office Bldg.
　Columbia, S. C. 29201

South Dakota
　Commissioner
　Office of Consumer Affairs
　Attorney General's Office
　State Capitol
　Pierre, S.D. 57501

Tennessee
　Attorney General
　State of Tennessee
　Supreme Court Bldg.
　Nashville, Tenn. 37219

Texas
　Assistant Attorney General and Chief
　Antitrust and Consumer Protection Division
　Capitol Station
　P.O. Box 12548
　Austin, Tex. 78711

　Commissioner
　Office of Consumer Credit
　1011 San Jacinto Blvd.
　P.O. Box 2107
　Austin, Tex. 78767

184

Consumer Frauds Division
Harris County Sheriff's Office
301 San Jacinto Blvd.
Houston, Tex. 77002

Utah
Assistant Attorney General for Consumer Protection
State Capitol
Salt Lake City, Utah 84114

Vermont
Assistant Attorney General
Consumer Protection Bureau
94 Church Street
Burlington, Vt. 05401

Virginia
Attorney General
Commonwealth of Virginia
Supreme Court-Library Bldg.
Richmond, Va. 23219

Administrator
Consumer Affairs
Department of Agriculture and Commerce
8th Street Office Bldg.
Richmond, Va. 23219

Washington
Deputy Attorney General and Chief
Consumer Protection and Antitrust Division
1266 Dexter Horton Bldg.
Seattle, Wash. 98104

West Virginia
Attorney General
State of West Virginia
The Capitol
Charleston, W. Va. 25305

Director
Consumer Protection Division
West Virginia Department of Labor
1900 Washington Street, East
Charleston, W. Va. 25305

Wisconsin
Attorney General
State of Wisconsin
Department of Justice
Madison, Wis. 53702

Director
Bureau of Consumer Protection
Department of Agriculture
801 West Badger Road
Madison, Wis. 53713

Wyoming
State Examiner and Administrator
Consumer Credit Code
State Supreme Court Bldg.
Cheyenne, Wyo. 82001

Index

187

Index

ABOUT THE AUTHOR

Sterling McLeod is a technical writer associated with a southwestern research laboratory. His interests cover a wide range of modern technology—from atomic energy to zoological research—and include, of course, consumer affairs.

Science Book Associates is an organization of writers and technical people active in many areas of science and technology. Their work in the preparation of audio-visual materials and training manuals to be used in science-oriented industry gives the editors an inside look at the developments that will affect the future.

381   McLeod, Sterling

        Careers in consumer
          protection

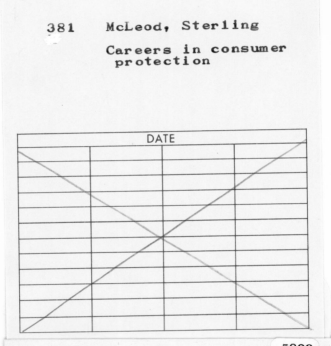

DATE			

© THE BAKER & TAYLOR CO.